Consultation in Gifted Education

Teachers Working Together to Serve Students

by Mary S. Landrum, Ph.D.

A special thank you goes to Joan Jacobs for her final reading of this book.

Creative Learning Press, Inc.
P.O. Box 320, Mansfield Center, CT 06250
888-518-8004 (phone) • 860-429-7783 (fax)
www.creativelearningpress.com • clp@creativelearningpress.com

Foreword

In 1996-98, the Charlotte-Mecklenberg Schools (CMS) in Charlotte, North Carolina, piloted a Resource Consultation and Collaboration Program named the Talent Development Program in ten elementary schools for two years. The program has extended to more than 25 elementary schools and an equal number of middle schools. I became the project consultant for the Talent Development Program and the contributing authors are staff members in the Charlotte-Mecklenburg Schools. Much of this book came from the collaborative efforts of the project consultant and program staff members, as well as contributions from parents and students. The ideas I present here evolved out of a need to address effectively and efficiently more students' needs.

I would like to acknowledge the hard work of many people in developing the comprehensive set of ideas about resource consultation in gifted education contained in this book. I also appreciate those leaders within the school district who possess a vision for an innovative approach to serving gifted learners. The CMS educators making the most contributions to this book are Sallie Dotson, Lea Harkins, Steve Houser, Betsy Moore, Sandra Payne, Jill Richardson, Jill Reicher, Lesley Spearman, and Carl Reid. When we began our journey together, we had only hope, each other, some initial ideas, and the desire to make it work. As a result, we believe that our efforts can be a road map for others. We hope that our efforts provide readers with guidelines and best practices for developing other resource consultation programs.

—*Mary Landrum, Ph.D.*

For more information on the research findings on the Talent Development Program, contact Mary Landrum at mlandrum@virginia.edu.

Table of Contents

List of Figures

Introduction

For more than two years, ten schools studied and implemented a program called the Resource Consultation and Collaboration Program. This program brought together general education and gifted education staff members to provide appropriately differentiated educational opportunities to gifted learners in grades K-6. The service delivery strategy built on the unique strengths and expertise of all staff members within the school and district at large, and when these strengths came together, the provision of appropriate educational intervention for gifted learners was enhanced. In essence, general education staff and specialists worked together to share responsibility for educating gifted learners.

* * *

Resource consultation and collaboration is becoming increasingly more popular as gifted education specialists consider alternative ways to serve gifted learners. It addresses many of the questions and concerns that have risen out of traditional service delivery models in gifted education.

- If giftedness is not static, why don't schools provide differentiation to children more often?
- How can schools offer gifted learners more challenging learning environments with their same-ability peers?
- Why must gifted learners leave the general education classroom for pull-out programs when it may not be the most appropriate time to do so?
- How can gifted education gain a more positive status among all educators?
- How can gifted learners gain access to a greater number of differentiated education services?
- How can gifted education and general education programs complement rather than compete with one another?
- How might general educators and gifted education specialists improve communication among themselves?
- Given current educational reforms, how might gifted education develop complementary service delivery strategies that complement rather than conflict with changes?

Consider the following: Pull-out programs tend to operate separately from regular education programs and serve students on a limited basis. This segregation of gifted services can contribute to perceptions of elitism, limit the transfer of learning, and serve gifted children's needs only some of the time. Gifted learners need intervention more than one or two times a week given that their unique characteristics and needs are not static. However, no one gifted education specialist would ever be able to serve the needs of these students all the time. Resource consultation and collaboration, in contrast, can bring more educators into the differentiated service model and increase the frequency of services being provided to gifted learners. Further, because the general educator is participating in the process, students can benefit from differentiation that extends and enhances the regular curriculum experience.

Collaborative efforts do not eliminate specialized services for gifted learners. Instead they redefine the role of a resource teacher from one in which he or she primarily provides direct service to students to one in which he or she provides both direct and indirect services (such as helping a regular classroom teacher pre-assess students' mastery levels in a content area). As a result of the Resource Consultation and Collaboration Program implemented in the 10 schools in which I was program consultant, gifted education specialists learned more about the general education program, while classroom teachers and other specialists became more familiar with the field of gifted education. Not only did educators benefit from this process, but students not formally identified as gifted also showed gains. When they demonstrated requisite mastery levels of the regular curriculum, these students participated in differentiated lessons inside and outside the regular classroom. In a traditional gifted education program, these students would not have been given opportunities to demonstrate their abilities or participate in differentiated lessons. Overall, schools sustained lasting positive effects on the school culture with shared responsibility and a collaborative atmosphere.

This handbook addresses how and why resource consultation and collaboration is done. It is meant to be a guidebook for understanding Resource Consultation and Collaboration Programs and a stimulus for developing similar programs.

Chapter 1

Overview of Resource Consultation & Collaboration Programs

*"I don't know who is formally identified [as gifted] anymore;
I just serve kids who need something different."—Classroom Teacher*

Resource consultation and collaboration rely on practices that pull together a school's human resources and expertise to serve students. Because applying these practices to gifted education is a relatively new concept, a knowledge base has grown out of other fields such as school psychology and special education. This chapter presents an overview of a Resource Consultation and Collaboration Program, including definitions, characteristics, purposes, basic tenets, goals and objectives, and benefits.

Definitions

Collaboration among specialists and general education school personnel allows teachers to meet the needs of gifted students in the general education classroom and improve education for all learners. When used to serve special needs students, this process is called "resource consultation." Similarly, M. Curtis and J. Meyers (1985) define "consultation" as a collaborative problem-solving effort through a sharing of expertise among two or more individuals with the ultimate goals of better serving students for whom they bear some level of responsibility. Applied to gifted education settings, resource consultation and collaboration are the processes whereby two or more school staff members share their expertise to plan and deliver differentiated education to gifted learners for whom they have some level of responsibility.

Characteristics

Resource Consultation and Collaboration Programs are identified by a number of characteristics (Cooke & Friend, 1991; Donovan, 1990) that distinguish it from more traditional types of service delivery in gifted education. First and foremost, collaboration and consultation practices are voluntary, suggesting that only when participants are able to select the processes as viable strategies are they successful. Second, no party involved in the processes should feel superior to the other. Consultation and collaboration, as discussed here, rely on the equally important but different expertise of participating individuals. The third characteristic of resource consultation is the focus on work-related issues in a collegial and professional atmosphere. Fourth, a context of confidential and authentic communication must exist among participants regarding issues at hand, the context and nature of the dialogue, as well as the efforts put forth by participants. Finally, participants provide direct services (services delivered directly to students without engaging in collaboration or consultation) as well as indirect services (provisions planned and implemented among colleagues that eventually eafect students).

Purposes

In general, the intent of resource consultation and collaboration is to allow educators to combine strengths in new ways to accomplish more for students. When applied to gifted education, these processes have several more specific purposes. One aim is to communicate among *all* school staff the educational programming for gifted learners. Furthermore, educators engage in consultation and collaboration for the purpose of team problem solving regarding the needs of highly-able students. In other words, school staffs engage in consultation with one another to plan, implement, and monitor differentiated educational opportunities for individual gifted learners.

Basic Tenets

The nature of collaborative efforts to provide appropriate educational experiences is inherently unique to the circumstances and contexts surrounding individual schools, staffs, and students. However, several universal tenets form the foundation for and guide the best practice of resource consultation as applied to the educating gifted learners.

First, all collaboration and consultation efforts should focus on providing *appropriate* educational opportunities to target students. Many gifted students become bored with lessons that are not appropriately challenging, and, as a result, some of these students may become behavioral problems in class. While collaboration and consultation efforts will address the problem of boredom in the classroom, educators should not see it as merely a way to discourage disruptive behavior. The differentiated activities—the appropriate educational opportunities that meet the needs and abilities of gifted students—that arise out of collaboration are the real purpose and focus of resource consultation and collaboration efforts, not ameliorating behavioral issues. In addition, collaboration and consultation should enhance, rather than diminish, existing school efforts regarding student intervention services. In other words, the collaborative process does not eliminate specialized intervention for gifted learners, but rather redefines the roles and responsibilities of school staffs in the provision of services. In fact, as regular classroom teachers get involved in planning and implementing differentiated activities, collaboration can help integrate general education programs and differentiated programs for gifted learners, providing a continuity and cohesiveness that is often lacking in traditional gifted programs.

Collaboration should also involve many school and community members, including administrators, support personnel, students, regular education teachers, specialists, central office personnel, parents, community leaders, and others. By including many individuals in program efforts, schools can take advantage of a variety of talents, strengths, and collective creativity and problem-solving skills. Finally, and perhaps most important, resource consultation and collaboration efforts should be flexible. Not only does the "what" (differentiated content) vary depending on the students, but the "who" and the "where" can change as well. Differentiated activities can take place with the classroom teacher, gifted education specialist, technology teacher, or supervised parent in the general education classroom, gifted education resource setting, or settings of support personnel. This flexibility leads to a spillover effect to the entire school. Because more personnel are involved and because personnel can be more creative in how they use school space, more students than those traditionally identified as gifted can receive services.

Goals and Objectives

The goals of resource consultation and collaboration in gifted education are fairly simple. Specialists and generalists combine efforts and expertise to accomplish more in the education of gifted learners. The participating staff become more knowledgeable and, therefore, more effective in their subsequent interactions with and instruction of gifted learners in their classrooms. Specific goals should be to (a) improve the efficacy of teacher instruction of and staff interaction with gifted students to improve students' education and (b) develop skills so that regular classroom teachers can sometimes work with gifted learners independently of the gifted education specialist (Donovan, 1990).

To obtain the target goals, particular procedural objectives must guide consultation and collaboration efforts. Foremost, general education staff and gifted education specialists engaging in collaboration and consultation *share responsibility* for designing educational services for gifted learners. Educators must focus on common needs that ignite collaboration and establish a *mutual dialogue* about providing educational services to gifted learners. Finally, the most important goal of collaboration and consultation is the ensuing *delivery of collaboratively planned learning activities* to gifted students. In short, shared responsibility focused on common needs leads to a mutual dialogue that promotes collaboratively planned and delivered educational experiences.

Benefits

Although resource consultation and collaboration is unique from application to application, there are a significant number of benefits to engaging in resource consultation and collaboration. One gifted education specialist in the Charlotte-Mecklenberg system reported of the program: " [It] allows me to focus on the strengths of each child. Several students I have this year work daily with the literacy teacher because they are below grade level in reading and other communication skills. However, these same students excel in mathematics. I can focus on these areas by planning and working with the classroom teacher to accommodate their needs through compacting and differentiating the instruction. This [attention to specific needs] would not happen in a pull-out program." Unlike traditional models for serving gifted children, resource consultation can benefit entire schools and raise the level of service for all students.

Program Benefits

1. Gifted education and general education are related, connected, and integrated.
2. The stigma of a pull-out program is minimized.
3. Differentiated education is child-focused.
4. More sophisticated content can be incorporated into differentiated lessons.
5. Pull-out or out-of-classroom sessions are scheduled when needed most.
6. Teachers and gifted education specialists can make more efficient use of instructional time.
7. The approach is easy to sell to parents.
8. A continuity exists between general education and differentiated activities.
9. Curriculum materials that complement the general education program are used for differentiation.
10. It is suitable for a site-based management approach, since each building develops unique applications.
11. The program promotes reduced teacher-student ratio during key instructional sessions.
12. Serving the needs of the same students is a common denominator among staff.
13. Staff members share accountability for continual student progress.
14. Frequency of differentiated activities increases.
15. Staff share a common educational language.
16. More and different staff become involved in the education of gifted learners.
17. Staff solidarity increases.

Staff Benefits

1. Teachers are less isolated.
2. Staff members increase communication among themselves.
3. Staff members share instructional responsibility.
4. Enthusiasm over collaboration carries over to other programs and staff.
5. Professional development opportunities for all staff members and parents evolve.
6. There is enhanced cooperation among staff and programs.
7. It encourages positive peer interactions among educators.
8. It enhances shared decision making among staff members.

9. School staff other than specialists participate in training in gifted education.
10. The program promotes mutual trust and respect.
11. Collaboration allows teaching to each group of diverse learners at once.
12. Teaching becomes more innovative.
13. Educators form strong teaching teams.
14. Staff members gain an enhanced knowledge of students' strengths and needs.
15. Staff creativity increases.

Student Benefits

1. Students can be held accountable for differentiated activities when they are included in regular classroom assessments.
2. The pace of learning is enhanced.
3. Gifted learners have more time together during differentiated instruction.
4. Non-identified students participate in some activities.
5. Pre-assessments lead to raising the ceiling on the regular education curriculum.
6. Student transition from general to gifted education is smooth.
7. Gifted students model higher-level thinking and creativity for other students in the classroom.
8. Several intervention specialists collaborate in the provision of services.
9. Students have more time for in-depth and sophisticated study.
10. Students' high potential can be addressed in the regular classroom setting as well as in gifted education resource settings.
11. At-risk students and those with specific aptitudes can be served in the regular classroom setting.
12. All students have instructional time together with other students of similar ability.

Anyone participating in the implementation of a Resource Consultation and Collaboration Program must possess a general understanding of the nature of resource consultation as well as the program's purposes, goals, and benefits. In order to gain the support of as many educators as possible as early as possible, those implementing a Resource Consultation and Collaboration Program should offer informational sessions that outline the goals and benefits of the program. Many will be won over by the benefits of the program and its focus on providing challenging educational opportunities to as many students as need it, not just a select few.

COMPONENTS OF RESOURCE CONSULTATION & COLLABORATION PROGRAMS

"This Resource Consultation Program is like having many hands all working toward the same goals."—Gifted Education Specialist

Resource Consultation Components

Resource Consultation Model

Only one resource consultation model has been readily applied to gifted education (Ward & Landrum, 1994), and the most unique aspect of this model is its primary goal to use limited and expensive resources effectively and efficiently. This hierarchical model consists of three levels of consultation (see Figure 2.1) (Curtis, Curtis, & Graden, 1988). At level one, general educators work together to develop provisions within the regular classroom to match the unique characteristics and needs of gifted learners. At level two, classroom teachers and gifted education specialists work together to plan and implement lessons and evaluate student learning for gifted students. Action taken at these two lower levels of the model are more economical than the next highest level and represent program efficiency and cost effectiveness. At level three, larger teams of school staff members get involved and pool their expertise, resources, and strengths to provide differentiated educational opportunities to gifted learners. Figure 2.2 outlines the nature of each level of the resource consultation model and presents sample consultative and collaborative activities in gifted education at each level of the model.

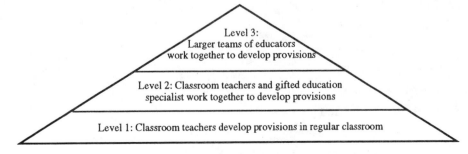

Level 3:
Larger teams of educators
work together to develop provisions

Level 2: Classroom teachers and gifted education
specialist work together to develop provisions

Level 1: Classroom teachers develop provisions in regular classroom

Figure 2.1. Hierarchy for consultation service delivery.

Resource Consultation Model Level	Sample Activities
LEVEL ONE: Collaboration among general educators.	• team teaching • intraclass grouping of students • grade-level planning for differntiation • sharing classroom materials and other resources
LEVEL TWO: Collaboration among general educators and the gifted education specialist with shared responsibility for gifted learners.	• integration of regular classroom and specialized instruction for gifted learners • collaborative teaching • consultation for differentiation • materials location, selection, and/or development • demonstration teaching by gifted education specialist • shared student assessment • joint parent-teacher confernces • curriculum planning
LEVEL THREE: Collaboration among teams or small groups (e.g., counselors, administrators, gifted education coordinator, teachers, etc.) to resolve issues regardinig the education of gifted learners.	• student identification • student placement • individualized educational planning • trouble-shooting • at-risk student identification, placement,services, and evaluation

Figure 2.2. Resource consultation activities in gifted education.

Resource Consultation Process

Dettmer, Thurston, and Dyck (1999) describe consultation and collaboration as activities among participants who communicate with one another about educational programming for all students; cooperate with one another in planning, implementing, and monitoring student learning; and coordinate all collaborative efforts that exist within a single educational program. These activities are the result of a highly specific consultation process that is the foundation of every Resource Consultation and Collaboration Program. Although there are many variations in the stages of the resource consultation process, Dettmer, Thurston, and Dyck (1999) have developed the most inclusive of all possible steps:

1. Prepare for the consultation
2. Initiate the consultation
3. Collect information
4. Isolate the problem
5. Identify the problem
6. Generate solutions
7. Formulate a plan
8. Evaluate process and progress
9. Follow-up on the situation
10. Repeat consultation as appropriate

Figure 2.3 illustrates this ten-step process. School staffs use this process (in some variation or in its entirety) to engage in a dialogue focused on a common problem for which the participants share responsibility. For example, a classroom teacher and gifted education specialist may meet to resolve a problem related to adapting core learning experiences during reading instruction. In addition to the classroom teacher and gifted education specialist, any teacher or specialist in the school or school division may be brought into the consultation process in order to determine possible modifications to instructional strategies and pace, curricular content, and student outcomes. From this dialogue, educators develop, implement, and follow up on mutually agreed upon services.

The resource consultation process—the two-way dialogue between consultant and consultee—must be learned, practiced, and refined. While at first the process may seem awkward and time-consuming, each time professionals come together, they repeat and refine this step-by-step process. Eventually it becomes a more efficient and natural part of the school day.

The Triad of Best Practice in Resource Consultation

Resource consultation involves three essential practices: co-planning, co-teaching, and follow-up. Co-planning requires that teachers come together to implement the consultation

---

Consultation Process

Classroom Teacher: Mrs. Brown recognizes that Jeremy, a third-grade student, finishes all of his work quickly. He seems to understand new ideas very quickly and yearns to move on. She realizes that she can't move the entire class at this advanced pace, but she feels that Jeremy shouldn't have to sit and wait for the other children to catch up. Mrs. Brown needs help. She gathers some of Jeremy's work and asks the gifted education teacher to meet with her briefly.

Gifted Education Specialist: Mr. Jones listens to Mrs. Brown's concerns and takes a look at Jeremy's classroom work. He asks several questions about Jeremy and Mrs. Brown's classroom.

Gifted Education Specialist: Mr. Jones arranges some individual achievement testing for Jeremy in math. He reports Jeremy's advanced achievement level to Mrs. Brown. They discuss several possible adaptations to math instruction in Mrs. Brown's classroom, and they explore ideas of accelerating Jeremy by moving him to a fourth-grade math lesson. They decide together what works best for everyone.

Gifted Education Specialist: Mr. Jones provides Mrs. Brown with some alternative instructional materials and together they work on a plan for implementation. The two teachers decide who will be responsible for each activity. They decide to evaluate Jeremy's performance together.

Classroom Teacher: Mrs. Brown checks with Mr. Jones once a week during her planning time to make minor adjustments in their plans and discuss Jeremy's progress.

Gifted Education Specialist: Mr. Jones and Mrs. Brown discuss how their collaboration has been working and develop more long-term plans for Jeremy's math studies for the remainder of the school year.

Classroom Teacher: Mrs. Brown has noticed several advanced readers in her classroom and contemplates meeting with Mr. Jones to consult and collaborate for the differentiation of these students' language arts studies.

Figure 2.3. Educators engaging in consultation.

process around a common need. Primarily, gifted education and classroom teachers co-plan, but other personnel are brought into the consultation process as needed. Co-planning is an on-going process that occurs regularly for at least 30 minutes a week (Landrum, 2001).

In collaborative teaching, the general education and gifted education specialists work together to implement lessons that they planned together. Even when instruction occurs at different times and in different places (resource room, classroom, media room, etc.) for each teacher involved, the teachers share responsibility for that instruction.

Follow-up involves two types of assessment: student and teacher. First, educators should come together to plan and implement assessment procedures for student products such as student performance or product rubrics and/or assigning grades for student efforts. The classroom teacher and gifted education specialist should share the assessment process by collaboratively assigning a single grade or assigning separate grades for differentiated work. Likewise, the participating educators should also assess their own performance and the effectiveness of resource consultation as they have implemented it. Educators should thoughtfully critique both co-planning and co-teaching and make suggestions for future implementations.

Collaboration and Consultation Activities

In any school, opportunities for consultation and collaboration are limitless, and each school will develop activities and patterns that are unique. However, certain program activities used in established Resource Consultation and Collaboration Programs can help teachers first beginning to practice consultation and collaboration in gifted education. Using these activities that have been known to be successful increases the chances that new programs will experience initial success as well. Following are a variety of activities that are particularly important in a Resource Consultation and Collaboration Program:

Team or grade-level co-planning sessions: The gifted education specialist joins the general education teachers' regular planning sessions to ensure that any differentiated learning activities they develop together are related to the regular curriculum. All student activities should be connected or interrelated to facilitate student transfer of learning.

Organizational needs (e.g., scheduling activities, grouping students for instruction, etc.): Gifted education specialists and general education teachers must communicate with each another about organizational needs, problems, and solutions that facilitate learning. Together they may decide which students will participate in individual differentiated lessons or adapt student schedules to create more time for in-depth study.

Student identification and placement: Gifted education specialists and classroom teachers should work with one another to identify students' unique learning needs in order to place students in appropriate groups. For example, the gifted education specialist might teach a demonstration lesson to an entire class in order for the classroom teacher to assess student behavior related to giftedness.

Instructional resource materials: After observing classrooms or discussing resource needs with classroom teachers, the gifted education specialist gathers and distributes materials for gifted learners to support classroom teaching. These materials may supplement or replace one classroom resource for another. For example, novels may be used to replace basal readers. Maps, encyclopedias, or CD-ROM materials may extend what is available to students through textbooks or supplant them entirely.

Differentiated learning activities and curriculum development: Although the gifted education specialist facilitates most differentiated learning activities through indirect or direct service delivery, these endeavors should develop out of consultation and/or collaboration between the gifted education specialist and general education teachers. Even if the gifted education specialist is solely responsible for developing and implementing certain curricula (e.g., direct services), the context of what is being taught or how something is being taught should result from collaboration and consultation. For example, a teacher could decide that advanced students need to read a more challenging text when studying science fiction during an upcoming curricular unit. The gifted education specialist chooses an appropriately challenging novel and communicates to students the expectations and requirements for the novel study. As a result of this co-planning, while regular classroom students read a particular novel for a language arts lesson, the advanced students read the more sophisticated novel from the same genre and participate in related but more challenging learning activities.

Independent studies and contracts: There are several ways in which classroom and gifted education specialists can collaborate and consult with one another to develop and manage students' independent studies and learning contracts. The gifted education specialist may design contracts and independent study projects that students work on outside the classroom, during designated classroom time, or both.   The gifted specialist and classroom teacher will jointly decide who will facilitate and monitor student progress.

Student progress and assessment: Teachers and gifted specialists collaboratively monitor student learning and share responsibility for evaluating student work and assigning grades. For example, the classroom teacher might focus on introducing new content to the students, while the gifted education specialist pre-assesses student performance or skill mastery in order to place students in appropriate instructional groups or for curriculum compacting. To assess students' differentiated learning outcomes, educators might collaboratively design and implement graduated rubrics.

Cooperative Teaching

Cooperative teaching, including team teaching, complementary teaching, supportive learning activities, parallel teaching, and station teaching, is an instrumental part of the Resource Consultation and Collaboration approach. Figure 2.4 presents the breakdown of various approaches to cooperative teaching.

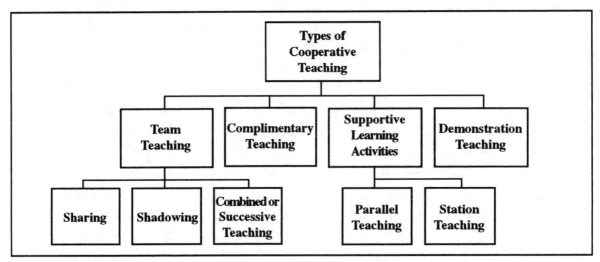

Figure 2.4. Types of cooperative teaching (adapted from Bauwens, Hourcade, and Friend, 1989).

Team Teaching

In team teaching educators work together to develop curricula and instruction and monitor student progress. Types of team teaching include sharing, shadowing, and combined or successive teaching (Bauwens, Hourcade, & Friend, 1989).

- *Sharing* places equal responsibility for the instruction of common gifted students on educators in gifted and general education. For example, the classroom teacher and gifted education specialist may divide tasks equally for a lesson or divide students into groups and each teach the same lesson
- *Shadowing* introduces the gifted education specialist into the general education classroom. After an introductory lesson to a new unit, the gifted education specialist may take a number of gifted students to the back of the classroom or to another room to conduct a differentiated lesson in the unit.
- In *Combined* or *Successive Teaching* general education teachers and gifted education specialists implement successive lessons. At the beginning of a unit, the gifted education specialist may plan to teach one novel to a group of gifted students while the classroom teacher teaches a different but related novel to a group of regular students.

Complementary Teaching

Complementary teaching involves separate but integrated teaching by instructors from the general and gifted education staffs. The gifted education specialist teaches knowledge and skills that complement the regular curriculum or that extend and enhance the regular curriculum. For example, the gifted education specialist could work with gifted learners for several math periods to teach problem-solving strategies that they could then practice on their own in the regular classroom during designated times.

Supportive Learning Activities

In supportive learning activities, the general educator is responsible for teaching content, and the gifted educator is responsible for designing student activities that support the content being taught but that are also more advanced and sophisticated for gifted learners. For example, the gifted education specialist may create enrichment activities or student contracts to supplement a particular unit taught in the regular classroom. Although the specialist is not involved in direct instruction, he or she has created materials that students will use at designated times in place of other classroom activities. There are two major types of supportive learning activities: parallel and station teaching (Dettmer, Dyck, and Thurston, 1999).

- *Parallel teaching* involves dividing the class into groups and delivering instruction that addresses the unique learning needs of each group. Students also receive differentiated instruction through supplemental learning activities. For example, the gifted education specialist could pull students out of classroom drill and practice activities to work on extension lessons that follow up on introductory lessons that the classroom teacher has taught.

- *Station teaching* requires that gifted education and general education teachers develop stations for student learning (e.g., interest centers, enrichment centers, and individualized learning contracts) that contain differentiated educational opportunities for gifted learners. Students visit the centers or work on contracts or extension activities related to a particular unit during designated times.

Demonstration Teaching

During demonstration teaching, gifted educators present lessons that illustrate to general educators how to differentiate lessons for gifted learners. Each lesson exhibits teacher skills and competencies related to the needs of gifted learners and helps provide teachers with the framework for making adaptations in the learning environment.

There are two primary goals for using demonstration lessons in a Resource Consultation and Collaboration program: (a) to heighten awareness of the needs of gifted learners and (b) to show examples of strategies for meeting those needs. When presenting a demonstration lesson, gifted specialists should provide the observing teacher with a written lesson plan and leave the teacher with follow-up activities for target students.

Some of the many benefits of demonstration lessons include:

- Gifted specialists and general educators gain practice and build comfort in working collaboratively.

- Classroom teachers are able to observe gifted behavior in students.

- Gifted specialists can observe and learn about the regular education classroom and curriculum.
- The classroom teacher has the opportunity to see differentiated instructional strategies in action.
- Teachers learn about one another's preferences and styles for teaching.

Figure 2.5 summarizes each type of cooperative teaching and Figure 2.6 presents an example of a cooperative teaching lesson.

Types of Cooperative Teaching	Summary Description
Team Teaching	The gifted education specialist and classroom teacher use sharing, shadowing, combined, or successive forms of teaching methods.
Complimentary Teaching	The gifted education specialist and classroom teacher teach separate but interrelated lessons.
Supportive Learning Activities	The classroom teacher determines content and the gifted education specialist designs supportive learning activities based on that content.
Demonstration Teaching	The gifted education specialist models for the classroom teacher best practice in curriculum and instruction differentiation in whole-class instruction.

Figure 2.5. Summaries of cooperative teaching styles.

Service Delivery

Indirect & Direct Services

Traditional gifted education services mainly involve direct services—those provisions developed and implemented by the gifted education specialist alone (Adams & Cessna, 1991). The gifted education specialist works directly with students without consulting or collaborating with anyone else. The Resource Consultation and Collaboration Program preserves direct services but minimizes the implementation of these efforts. Collaborative and consultative approaches place an emphasis on indirect services, and direct services are considered only when collaboration is not feasible. Any service that gifted education specialists and other teachers or specialists co-plan and co-teach is considered indirect. These services include provisions for gifted learners that are prepared and delivered in the general education classroom as well as lessons delivered in a specialist's area or resource room. Both types of service delivery roles are critical to the consultative and collaborative processes.

Direct Service Delivery Roles

The goal of resource consultation in gifted education is a combination of direct and indirect service delivery. In each case, the role of the gifted education teacher is different from

Animal Habitat Research Project

Purpose: To use a collaborative approach in teaching gifted elementary students that meets the goals of the regular classroom teacher, media specialist, and the gifted education specialist.

Format: Interclassroom grouping of high ability language arts students.

Objectives:
1. (Science) To study animal adaptations.
2. (Social Studies) To study North Carolina geography.
3. (Research) To study primary and secondary sources through technology.
4. (Higher Order Thinking) To use complex problem-solving skills with an emphasis on real-world problems.

Description: Fourth grade students research animal adaptations and habitats of animals that reside in the four biomes of North Carolina.

Steps:
1. The classroom teachers teach units on animal adaptations and North Carolina geography. The gifted education specialist collaborates with the teachers in developing these lessons.
2. The media specialist reviews research skills that students learned in past research projects.
3. Students each draw a card containing the name of an animal and its biome that they will research. There are four groups of approximately seven students. After students finish individual research on their animals, each biome group will complete a group project.
4. Each student receives six note cards to record information from each of the following areas: (a) description, (b) diet, (c) behavior, (d) threatening forces, (e) habitat, and (f) other information.
5. Students work in each of the four areas in the media center to research their animals: reference book area, periodical area, search screen and nonfiction area, and computer area. Groups rotate through these centers over the course of several days. The collaborating teachers are located at these centers to offer assistance and ask questions to enhance the depth of the project.
6. Each biome group meets and chooses a chairperson. The group paints a mural of its biome and places its animals in their appropriate places on the mural. The chairperson oversees the project and has the final say, should any controversies arise. The painting must be accurate in detail and description, and it must be based on research.
7. Having become an expert on his or her animal, each student creates a computer drawing using Kidpix® Computer Software of the animal in its natural habitat.
8. Each student saves his or her drawing, and each group compiles all of its drawings in a slideshow. There will be four slideshows, each focusing on one of the four biomes of North Carolina.
9. Using note cards for reference, each student prepares a thirty-second oral presentation sharing his or her research and adds it to the biome slideshow, making it a complete educational program.
10. The slideshows are recorded onto a videotape/disk.

Facilitation: Collaborating teachers are actively on hand to support and instruct, and students can complete the project in ten days by meeting for a class period each day. By working together, teachers are able to meet their individual curriculum goals and provide an enriched learning experience for students.

Figure 2.6. Sample collaborative lesson.

more traditional service delivery models that employ mostly direct services. In traditional gifted education programs, direct service delivery involves the gifted education specialist taking sole responsibility for providing educational experiences directly to gifted learners without consulting or collaborating with others.

In a Resource Consultation and Collaboration Program, the gifted education specialist may have a variety of direct services delivery roles, but these services are quite different from those provided in a traditional program. Although the specialist delivers direct services to students alone, co-planning and follow-up with classroom teachers may occur. In one type of direct service, the gifted education specialist plans and directs differentiated learning activities for pull-out sessions that complement the regular education curriculum. These lessons might involve coordinating interdisciplinary studies for gifted learners based on several academic areas of study in the core curriculum (e.g., mathematics, language arts, science, social studies, etc.).

Gifted education specialists may also conduct complementary or parallel teaching lessons that focus on helping students develop specific strategies that they can then apply to the core curricula when participating in regular education activities. For example, parallel lessons for gifted learners might focus on teaching students higher order process skills through critical thinking training programs. Students can then apply the skills to differentiated activities that they pursue in the regular classroom.

Not all direct services involve the gifted education specialist standing in front of a group of students delivering instruction outside of the regular classroom. The specialist can deliver direct services to target students by developing and providing learning centers for the regular classroom and monitoring student progress in center activities. Although the classroom teacher may have input into the center's connection with the regular curriculum, he or she is not responsible for student learning.

Gifted education specialists can also provide direct services that lead to student identification and placement in specialized programming for gifted learners. If gifted education specialists teach differentiated lessons to students in the regular classroom, then all students have the opportunity to develop their potential in an environment conducive to giftedness. With opportunities to pursue a topic more deeply or extend their thinking, some students may then achieve at levels not seen in standardized testing or when activities are not sufficiently challenging. Showing this potential, these students then may be formally identified as gifted and placed in differentiated educational services for gifted learners. (This type of direct service can become important when gifted programming receives funding based on the number of formally identified students.)

Indirect Service Delivery Roles

When the gifted education specialist and the classroom teacher plan and deliver indirect services, they share responsibility for student learning. Indirect services involve educators jointly planning, teaching, and engaging in follow-up activities, and the services can take many forms. For example, the gifted education specialist can provide information or training to classroom teachers or other school staff personnel on how to use specific curricular or instructional best practices in the field of gifted education. Instead of providing direct instruction to students, the gifted education specialist works with other educators to show them how to provide appropriate instruction to gifted learners. A variation on this type of staff development occurs when the specialist conducts demonstration lessons in colleagues' classrooms. While students are getting direct instruction from the specialist, the underlying purpose of such lessons is to model best practices in providing differentiated instruction for high-end learning.

Another type of indirect service involves the gifted education specialist assisting classroom teachers with differentiating the curriculum for all students, including gifted learners. The gifted education specialist might first observe students and/or teachers in the regular classroom in order to learn more about the instructional environment, the curriculum, and the needs of gifted learners. Subsequently, the gifted education specialist joins classroom teachers during their planning time to provide them with ideas for curriculum development and instructional design. Likewise, the gifted education specialist might engage in a problem-solving session with a team of general educators as they work to individualize educational experiences for a particular gifted learner who needs acceleration. The gifted education specialist might also assist classroom teachers' efforts to support differentiated activities in their classrooms by gathering and/or creating instructional resources and materials that classroom teachers can use with gifted students.

Collaborative teaching in any format is considered an indirect service. For example, the gifted education specialist may assist classroom teachers with compacting student curriculum studies by providing supporting learning activities for gifted learners to do in the regular classroom with the time they have "bought out." Other co-teaching efforts include planning and directing gifted learners' independent studies and learning contracts and developing learning and/or interest centers for classroom teachers' use.

All collaborative follow-up activities to co-teaching are considered indirect services. Following most co-teaching efforts, the gifted education specialist should engage in assessment activities along with the classroom teacher and other participating specialists (e.g., the literacy teacher). The gifted education specialist can assist classroom teachers in monitoring student progress by developing and providing differentiated assessment rubrics. These rubrics ensure continuous learning for students at all ability levels, including gifted learners.

In order to support differentiated educational experiences for gifted learners, the gifted education specialist also often acts as a liaison between general educators, parents, educational support staff, administrators, and students. This type of indirect service can involve discussing gifted education scheduling and organizational needs with school administrators. Support for differentiation must also include organizing intra- and interclassroom groupings of students for instructional periods by assessing student readiness. Additionally, the gifted education specialist might coordinate student movement into and out of classrooms for partial or full acceleration. In all of these indirect services, the gifted education specialists and classroom teachers share responsibility for providing appropriate education experiences to gifted students.

In most traditional models of gifted education, resource teachers in gifted education have provided direct services to gifted learners on a part-time basis. Schedules allow the gifted education specialist to provide only direct differentiated educational opportunities to gifted learners in as little as an hour to as much as a day per week. A Resource Consultation and Collaboration Program in gifted education does not do away with these direct services, but it redefines the role of the resource teacher to include both direct and indirect service delivery roles and lays emphasis on indirect or collaborative services. The combination of services that involves activities in the regular classroom as well as the resource room provides more full-time attention to students' giftedness. Based on the success in established programs, I recommend that gifted education specialists spend 70% of their time involved in indirect services and 30% of their time involved in direct services (Landrum, 2001). Figure 2.7 contains sample role delineations for school staff involved in both direct and indirect services.

Classroom Teacher's Roles	Gifted Education Specialist's Roles	Shared Roles
• Identify performance standards and skills • Identify curriculum goals • Conduct student pretesting • Organize differentiated lessons	• Develop differentiated curriculum • Organize differentiated lessons • Organize resource materials • Develop interest centers • Develop work schedules • Manage overall workload	• Curriculum compacting • Co-teaching • Co-planning • Develop interest centers • Develop student contracts • Manage independent studies • Evaluate student work • Determine student grouping

Figure 2.7. Teacher roles in a Resource Consultation and Collaboration Program.

Student Grouping Practices

Grouping students for instruction is one of the most significant factors in the success of Resource Consultation and Collaboration Programs. Not only does it facilitate consultative and collaborative processes by limiting the number of professional relationships the gifted education specialist must establish and maintain, but it also creates conducive environments for appropriately differentiated curriculum and instruction. Appropriate groupings can foster higher-level thinking, debate, discussion, problem-solving, and decision-making by allowing high-ability students to move along the learning continuum at a common, advanced pace as compared with their same-age peers. However, grouping alone does little to further the education of gifted learners. Although gifted learners benefit from spending time with their mental peers, it is what is done during this time that is most important in their education. Differentiated educational opportunities must accompany appropriate strategies for grouping students.

There are a variety of ways to group students to make the most of instructional time, and collaborative efforts can increase the grouping possibilities. Self-contained classrooms, cluster grouping, intraclass grouping, and interclass grouping are the most typical grouping patterns for gifted students. Figure 2.8 outlines the benefits of these grouping strategies in a Resource Consultation and Collaboration Program.

Self-contained classrooms: Although no group of gifted students is completely homogeneous, there are common needs and instructional outcomes shared by all students. In self-contained classrooms, students of similar ability and, therefore, similar instructional needs are placed together. These children tend to stay together for the entire day, allowing the teacher to modify and adapt the curriculum and instruction in all disciplines.

Cluster grouping: Clusters consist of groups of 8-12 students of similar ability placed in a classroom with other children. When used most effectively, the other students in the classrooms are of average to above average ability. More than one cluster of students with specialized needs in one classroom is often extremely taxing on the teacher.

Intraclass grouping: Intraclassroom grouping involves moving students within a classroom into different group formations during instruction. These groups remain flexible so that students can move into and out of groups as their mastery levels and learning needs change. This type of grouping works best when students in the classroom logically fit into specific instructional groups. While the specific number of groups in a classroom can vary in terms of teacher competence and comfort levels, too many different groups are cumbersome and difficult to manage.

Interclass grouping: Interclassroom grouping draws on similar ability students groups across several classrooms at a grade level and places them together in one classroom for particular units of study. Students are re-grouped and distributed to classrooms in which teachers direct instruction to their level of performance and resulting needs. Groups remain flexible so that students' needs can be assessed and re-assessed and educators can adjust grouping. When students are not involved in major instructional lessons, students return to heterogeneous homeroom classrooms.

Grouping Strategies	Benefits of Grouping Strategy
Self-Contained Classroom	• Gifted education specialist has a fixed number of classroom teachers with whom to collaborate and consult. • Students can interact with same-ability peers all day.
Cluster Grouping	• Gifted education specialist has a fixed number of classroom teachers with whom to collaborate and consult. • Students can interact with same-ability peers all day.
Interclassroom Grouping	• Students can be grouped with same-ability peers. • Flexibility allows students to move in and out of instruction groups as needed. (Best accomplished by pretesting students.)
Intraclassroom Grouping	• Students can interact with same-ability peers in other classrooms. • Students can participate in a large group of gifted learners when all classrooms are pooled together.

Figure 2.8. Benefits of grouping strategies in a Resource Consultation and Collaboration Program.

The Gifted Education Specialist's Workload

Although there are many benefits to collegial collaborations, they are time-consuming and require effort. The frequency and number of collaborative partnerships are limited by the amount of available time and energy that both classroom teachers and gifted specialists have. As participants refine skills and become comfortable with the process, collaborative endeavors can increase. However, if educators are not careful, the overall number and frequency of these efforts could swallow an entire school day. Similarly, a high number of participants limits the flexibility of the gifted education specialist's work schedule, inhibiting the spontaneous nature of some of these activities. Therefore, an administrator knowledgeable about resource consultation processes should monitor the gifted education specialist's workload lest it become overwhelming. As a rule, in grades K-5 no gifted education specialist is able to work with more than two teachers per grade level without losing some effectiveness. Likewise, no more than twelve teachers from two different buildings assigned to one gifted education specialist are feasible.

There are several strategies for managing the collaboration workload within a school. Perhaps most important is delicately balancing the number of classrooms that any one gifted education specialist must serve. Rather than putting a few gifted students in every classroom, clustering students within classrooms or pooling students across classrooms into one group limits the number of classroom teachers involved in the collaboration process.

Establishing team planning sessions can also reduce the gifted education specialist's workload. Team planning limits the number of meetings between the resource teacher and individual general education teachers for planning and evaluating collaboration efforts. If teachers cannot come together as a team, then individual teachers should act as liaisons for other grade level teachers. Further, taking time for long-term planning can help the gifted education specialist draw up a master schedule of collaboration activities for extended periods of time. In these long-term planning schedules, the specialist should work to develop a balance of indirect and direct services. This balance minimizes the number of face-to-face contacts with resource and general education teachers, yet it provides services to students consistently over time.

Administrative Support

Administrative support is essential to the efficacy of a Resource Consultation and Collaboration Program. Administrators must be good advocates for the program and able and willing to articulate the program's philosophy, the nature of shared responsibility of all staff for all children, including gifted learners, and the importance of collaborative planning and teaching. Strong administrators will lend credibility to the program by visibly participating in it and will ensure program durability by providing continuing support to all educators involved in the program. Specific administrator support activities vary from school to school, but there are several crucial support services that administrators can provide.

Perhaps most important to establishing a strong foundation that supports consultation and collaboration is developing an appropriate schedule. First and foremost, in order for teachers to work together, they must have time to work with one another regarding appropriate educational decision-making, instructional practice, curriculum development, and student assessment. Administrators must develop work schedules that include a regularly appropriated time for staff members to consult and collaborate with one another. In addition, establishing class, grade level, and special program schedules conducive to consultation and collaboration practices can go a long way to determining the success of a Resource Consultation and Collaboration Program. Often teachers are all scheduled to teach one subject at the same time, making it difficult for the gifted education specialist to work with more than one teacher or one class at a time. For example, the entire school might engage in reading during the same time. Because the gifted education specialist can be in only one place at a time, he or she is limited in either the kind of service he or she provides or the number of classrooms in which he or she can serve. If the gifted education specialist needs to provide activities or instruction that raises the level of challenge for students across the grade level, he or she cannot provide anything that requires direct instruction to or monitoring of students when all those classes are scheduled for the same time slot. Because co-planning and co-teaching are an integral part of a Resource Consultation and Collaboration Program, the administrator must structure work schedules and instruction times so that these activities can take place regularly.

Just as scheduling practices can limit a gifted education specialist's efforts, poorly planned student grouping practices can spread a gifted education specialist too thin. Administrators should work to establish student grouping structures in and across classrooms that minimize the number of classrooms and teachers with whom any given gifted education specialist must be in direct contact. If the gifted education specialist can spend more time with only one or a few teachers (instead of attending to many teachers' different needs and classrooms), he or she will be able to provide better quality services more frequently.

Even after administrators tackle the task of developing workable schedules and appropriately assigning students to specific classrooms, the program will founder if administrators do not make technical assistance in resource consultation and collaboration practices available to target teachers. Initial staff development that focuses on the nature and context of consultation and collaboration practices is crucial, as is subsequent access to technical assistance in developing the processes and putting them into practice. As part of staff development, administrators should develop incentives for program participation. To be most effective, incentives should match specific participants' needs. For example, release time for training or planning can motivate teachers who want to collaborate but need time for long-range planning and materials development. Similarly, providing supplemental resource materials that support differentiation can also be an incentive to teachers who want to initiate their own differentiated activities after consulting with the gifted education specialist.

Like any new program a school pursues, Resource Consultation and Collaboration Programs involve large commitments of time and effort up front. However, grounding educators in the program's processes and activities and careful and deliberate planning establishes a strong foundation and makes the collaboration process easier, more inviting, more productive, and more efficient.

Implementing a Resource Consultation & Collaboration Program in Gifted Education

"It's like boot camp at the beginning . . . No one was more surprised than me
when I looked back and saw what we had accomplished."—Gifted Education Specialist

Getting Started

Consultation and collaboration processes are built on a foundation: the school. Getting to know the school (schedule, administration, staff, and curriculum) is an important first step in being able to collaborate with staff members. Often resource teachers in gifted education are limited in what they know about general education issues. Likewise, many classroom teachers know very little about what the gifted education specialist or the gifted program does for students. Therefore, it is important for all educators and administrators to visit classrooms and resource areas and talk with each other and students about the school and its programs. Educators will know they are ready to start collaboration and consultation when they have answered the questions in Figure 3.1.

Collaboration at a school-wide level is essential. When schools require gifted education specialists to devote themselves to collaboration and consultation activities while still maintaining existing service delivery formats, staff members find the paradigm shift challenging and difficult. The change is made more easily when schools abandon old service delivery

---

Initial Questions

1. Can I co-teach with someone?
2. How can we demonstrate students' mastery level of the general curriculum?
3. Will I work in the classrooms or pull out children to another learning area?
4. How can I buy time for more in-depth studies?
5. Which classrooms, instructional areas, and curriculum are best suited for consultation and collaboration?
6. What potential materials and resources are available in the school and the community?
7. How does the school schedule impact the consultation and collaboration processes?
8. Do I have time scheduled for delivering direct and indirect services, planning, and co-teaching?

Figure 3.1. Questions to answer before implementing a Resource Consultation and Collaboration Program.

models and embrace the new model wholeheartedly. The model is developed and sustained only when it is deemed the most appropriate service delivery model at the time of implementation.

Making Initial Contacts

Based on experiences in the Charlotte-Mecklenberg School District, the gifted education specialist[1] for the school is the best candidate for initiating resource consultation and collaboration processes and getting a program started. Many classroom teachers are not familiar enough with the gifted programming in a school district to know which questions or needs to address first. Initially, the gifted education specialist may want to approach teachers who already have some experience or interest in collaboration. However, if no such experienced individual is available, the gifted education specialist may choose to start out on friendly ground by working with a friend or acquaintance. Someone with whom there is an existing collegial relationship may be willing to try a new service delivery model, given the trust and comfort already established.

When working with people with whom there is no existing collegiality, the gifted education specialist should first extend invitations to join the collaborative process. Instead of establishing an immediate mandate to change, inviting people to participate allows potential participants to feel that they have a personal say and stake in the program.

To reach teachers reluctant to change to a new program, gifted education specialists might approach these teachers about a problem they think can be resolved through collaboration. Because many classroom teachers don't know enough about the specialist's area and where he or she can be of help, it falls to the gifted education specialist to bridge the gap by visiting classrooms and observing student behavior and instructional activities to generate solutions to problems and ideas for collaboration. For example, a teacher may have students who work at such rapid paces through existing curriculum that they become bored and sometimes act out in class and disturb other students. Raising the level of challenge in the curriculum and allowing students to move at their own rate of learning will decrease these negative behaviors. Being able to resolve a behavioral problem gives reluctant or unconvinced teachers a reason to seek collaborative and consultative support.

To show teachers the benefits of a Resource Consultation and Collaboration Program and how it can help them in their classrooms, the specialist should also visit grade-level planning sessions. Upon gaining familiarity with students and the curriculum, the specialist can offer a menu of possible collegial activities in which teachers and the specialist could engage. The gifted education specialist might also encourage unsure classroom teachers to visit co-planning sessions or classrooms in which collaborative activities are already taking place. They can then see the process in action and ease concerns about their own participation. For those most

---

[1] Throughout this section, I portray the gifted education specialist as the initiator of collaboration given what typically occurs in practice. Readers should note that the gifted programming administrator for the school or district could also be the one to initiate a program.

reluctant to participate in consultation and collaboration, gifted education specialists may offer to teach a demonstration lesson in a teacher's classroom. The classroom teacher typically likes this approach and is won over because of the nonthreatening and inclusive nature of this type of co-teaching. However, the gifted education specialist should be careful, as it is easy for classroom teachers to become overly complacent with this form of collaborative teaching, which demands little effort on their part to implement.

Making the Rounds

Whenever possible, the gifted education specialist should walk around the building to analyze what is happening during the day and generate ideas for collaborative efforts. While observing specific classes, the specialist may develop an idea to create extension lessons for a particular unit that a teacher is using or come up with a list of resource materials that support differentiated learning for target gifted learners. In addition, observing student behavior in classrooms helps identify and place students in specialized services. When making the rounds, the gifted education specialist is looking for answers to the following questions:

- How do gifted learners respond to the general education curriculum and classrooms?
- How do student diversity and learning differences impact instruction in the classroom?
- What curricular areas will be coming up at various grade levels?
- Which students might be gifted but have not been identified as such?
- Where are there mutual concerns and interests that may lend themselves to consultation and collaboration in the future?

Initial Activities

Armed with the answers to these questions, the gifted education specialist can begin to schedule activities that will "test the waters" and take the first steps toward developing a Resource Consultation and Collaboration Program. First, the gifted education specialist should schedule and conduct demonstration lessons on a regular basis in the same classroom. Upon observing any regular classroom lesson, the gifted education specialist plans a differentiated rubric for student products for an upcoming lesson. The next step is for educators to plan activities that lead to that differentiated rubric. Third, the gifted education specialist listens to the concerns of reluctant participants. Finally, participating educators should obtain administrative support for making appropriate changes to the organization of the school to establish a supportive environment.

Once the gifted education specialist has contacted colleagues intending to collaborate, the specialist and involved staff should conduct weekly co-planning sessions. Early sessions tend to focus on individual collaboration activities. However, after establishing weekly co-planning sessions, educators should seek administrative support for scheduling a long-term planning day to map content for the year. The long-term planning session allows weekly short-term sessions to become focused on the day-to-day maintenance of long-term plans.

Participants must remember that comprehensive and effective Resource Consultation and Collaboration Programs take time to build. It takes one to two years to fully implement a program. Starting small and making small gains through steady and continuous progress ensures success.

Parent Communication

After taking the first steps toward establishing a Resource Consultation and Collaboration Program, school staffs must communicate with parents about the program and the benefits the service delivery model offers to students, especially if the new program involves significant changes to existing gifted education services. Foremost, educators must address the expected outcomes and timeline for implementation of the program, and an initial meeting of parents and staff is recommended. It is critical that schools gain support from parents, keep them informed about efforts to serve students, and get them involved in collaborations. To establish and maintain communication and support, schools can create parent orientation programs, send newsletters and letters, put together work portfolios, and schedule parent meetings and conferences. Figure 3.2 presents two letters that communicate program activities to parents.

Planning

Systematic and recurring planning sessions are imperative to a Resource Consultation and Collaboration Program. Planning sessions foster discussions about common goals and needs

---

Letter One

Dear Parents,

The gifted education programming in the school district has expanded to include your child's classroom. The program is called Catalyst and allows children to challenge their areas of giftedness more often and in a variety of settings.

The gifted and talented students at each grade level have been placed in cluster groups in specified regular education classrooms in grades 3-5. The teachers of these classrooms will work collaboratively with me to serve gifted and talented students in the classrooms. Other children who demonstrate existing mastery of current educational objectives will be included in differentiated educational opportunities as well.

In this model, your child will work on challenging educational opportunities that are built on or extend from the regular education program, giving your child an opportunity to learn beyond what is presented in the regular curriculum. This differentiated work promotes learning at faster rates, thinking at higher levels, and studying sophisticated and complex content.

We look forward to serving your child this year and hope that you will join us in our efforts to provide quality educational opportunities.

Sincerely,

The Gifted Education Specialist

Figure 3.2. Sample parent letters.

Letter Two

Dear Parent,

I have thoroughly enjoyed working with your child this year. McKee is one of several schools in the school district that provides a Resource Consultation and Collaboration Program for serving gifted and high-ability students. In this approach, students are pulled out of their regular classroom activities to receive the services of the gifted teacher.

I regularly join the math-science teacher in teaching lessons that involve higher level thinking skills, complex problem-solving skills, real-world problems, and special projects. Although my focus is on helping students become good thinkers, my lessons support the curriculum goals of the school district and the benchmark goals of each grade level at our school.

In the fourth grade, we often used the outdoors as our classroom while we studied animal adaptations. I collaborated with the media specialist to develop a research project that involved extracting reference information from computer programs as well as from books. We also learned about gravity as we worked with toys that were on board the space shuttle. Hands-on work with Lego®s gave us insights into the operations of simple machines. I attempted to provide direct services to your child at least once a week, and I hope your child told you weekly of the many activities we undertook. If not, ask about the rocket launch, the tracking lessons, and study of compounds and mixtures, too.

In the third grade, we studied the interdependence of plants and animals. I collaborated with the media specialist to develop a research project that involved extracting reference information from computer programs as well as from books. We learned about compounds and mixtures as we tasted interesting concoctions and tried to identify them. Hands-on work with Lego®s gave us insights into how we use different energy sources to make our lives easier. I attempted to provide direct services to your child at least once a week. While I have mentioned only few activities, I hope your child told you weekly of the many activities we undertook. If not, ask about the 17 lb. "gold" nugget that we examined, the "tree" that the class created together, or the electrical circuits that we made.

In the second grade, I came into the classrooms on a weekly basis and worked directly with students during their math-science time. We often went outside to study the characteristics of plants and animals. I collaborated with the media specialist to develop a research project that involved learning how to take notes and prepare a report. We learned about our talents and of the eight documented intelligences. While we are very talented as humans, we also learned that birds have the ability to make a nest that is better than the ones that we tried to make from natural objects. These examples are a few of our undertakings, and I hope your child kept you informed of the other lessons that were our foci.

We have had an excellent year. We hope you will have a terrific summer.

Sincerely,

Gifted Education Specialist

Figure 3.2. Sample parent letters (cont.).

and allow educators to plan for cooperative teaching, division of responsibility, evaluation, and grouping and to report on the progress of shared students and their differentiated learning activities. Schools need to set aside half-day or full-day planning sessions at least twice a year for long-term planning. These sessions allow staff time to reflect and create with one another and build collaboration into the entire school year. This type of long-term planning is critical to the gifted education specialist who must juggle a schedule that includes several colleagues.

Additionally, teachers and other educators must have time built into their weekly schedules to engage in consultation and collaboration. Teachers and the gifted education specialist need to meet at least once a week to maintain long-term plans, monitor progress toward common goals, and make short-term plans for collaboration or to consult with one another. This planning time should be a true constant built into the regular school day (as opposed to educators grabbing a few moments between lessons or meeting before or after school).

For planning time to be programmed into the gifted education specialist's schedule, it is important to coordinate his or her schedule around existing grade-level planning times. If the specialist's schedule is built in with existing planning sessions and around personal planning time, then both planning periods are protected from being displaced by on-going requests from individual teachers for collaboration and consultation. If common or grade-level planning does not exist and individual requests for planning sessions threaten to consume a specialist's schedule, one classroom teacher per grade level or department should meet with the gifted education specialist and report back to other teachers. The teacher who meets with the specialist becomes a liaison to other teachers on the same grade level or in that department.

Perhaps one of largest problems schools face as they establish planning or inservice sessions for teachers is finding qualified teacher substitutes. Because release time remains one of the most effective incentives for teachers to engage in consultation and collaboration activities, administrators must find alternative approaches to hiring substitutes. For example, administrators may decide to recruit supervised community volunteers to provide classroom teachers and specialists release time for planning. As administrators and educators develop schedules, the issue of covering educators' time out should be an integral part of the plan.

Documentation

Planning sessions often generate a flurry of ideas, tasks, timelines, and other details. A resource teacher may have a number of these sessions on any given day and could easily become overwhelmed with information. As a result, educators must record their plans for differentiated educational opportunities. A written record will guide the implementation of these efforts as well as assist the gifted education specialist in organizing his or her activities across many grade levels and individual classrooms. In addition, the plan becomes a permanent record of these important activities. To keep the process simple, participants can develop a form and duplicate it to use at all planning sessions. Figure 3.3 contains a sample form for recording information during planning sessions.

Figures 3.4-3.13 in the following pages present several formats (both blank and completed) for documenting plans for curricular and instructional differentiation. Figures 3.14-3.16 contain monthly documentation forms for all collaboration and consultation efforts.

Documenting differentiated learning outcomes for each activity is just as important as documenting plans. The documentation helps teachers and students recognize the challenge

---

Gifted Education Specialist Contact

Teacher:_____   Date:_____

Content Area(s):_____

_____

_____

Requests/Questions/Concerns:_____

_____

_____

_____

_____

_____

_____

_____

_____

Figure 3.3. Sample planning session documentation form.

level of each learning activity and the expectations for student products. Further, parents need to have an indication of differentiated learning opportunities in which their children have been involved. A simple icon on each activity can serve to identify differentiated learning activities (Dettmer, Thurston, & Dyck, 1993). One school labels differentiated activities with a large "PG" (for Programs for the Gifted). This distinction is very important to parents who are not aware of the specific times that their children are engaged in differentiated learning experiences. In other models of gifted education, service is prescribed for a certain day and time, and parents are aware of the times when their children are receiving differentiated educational experiences. In contrast, a Resource Consultation and Collaboration Program does not have hard and fast rules about who receives services and when they receive them, and a collection of identified materials may become the only record of differentiated learning experiences for some students.

Lesson Planner

Theme:_____

Generalization:_____

Literature:_____

_____

Writing:_____

_____

Vocabulary:_____

_____

Art:_____

_____

Math:_____

_____

Science:_____

_____

Social Studies:_____

_____

Culminating Activity:_____

_____

Field Trips/Resources/Etc.:_____

_____

Evaluation:_____

_____

Timeline:_____

_____

Figure 3.4. Blank lesson planning form.

Lesson Planner

Theme: Systems

Generalization: Systems have inputs, outputs, and interrelationships.

Literature:

Writing:

Vocabulary:

Art:

Math:

Science: PowerPoint presentations on the Mimi

Social Studies:

Culminating Activity: Panel discussion on environmental issues

Field Trips/Resources/Etc.: Work with technology teacher

Evaluation: Differentiated rubric for PowerPoint presentation

Timeline: In-class work and two science lessons per week for three weeks

---

Figure 3.5. Completed lesson planning form.

Student Differentiation Plan

Student Name:_____ Grade Level:_____

Classroom Teacher:_____

Gifted Education Specialist:_____

Program Status: Non-gifted_____ Gifted_____

Strengths	Documentation	Differentiation
Math	____Pre-assessment ____85%ile Achievement ____Creative Problem Solver ____Critical Thinker ____Grades of A or B ____Proficiency Scores	
Communication	____Pre-assessment ____85%ile Achievement ____Creative Problem Solver ____Critical Thinker ____Grades of A or B ____Proficiency Scores	
Social Studies		
Science		

Figure 3.6. Blank student differentiation plan.

Student Differentiation Plan		

Student Name: Jane Doe   Grade Level: 3

Classroom Teacher:

Gifted Education Specialist:

Program Status: Non-gifted___X___ Gifted_____

Strengths	Documentation	Differentiation
Math	_X_ Pre-assessment ____ 85%ile Achievement _X_ Creative Problem Solver _X_ Critical Thinker _X_ Grades of A or B ____ Proficiency Scores	• Hands-on Equations • Hawk Measurement Unit • Photo Math Lesson • Problem-Solving Project
Communication	____ Pre-assessment ____ 85%ile Achievement ____ Creative Problem Solver ____ Critical Thinker ____ Grades of A or B ____ Proficiency Scores	
Social Studies		
Science		

Figure 3.7. Completed student differentiation plan.

Differentiated Curriuclum Planner Grade Level:_____				
Discipline	**September**	**October**	**November**	**December**
Science				
Math				
Literature				
Communications				
Social Studies				
Interdisciplinary Units				
Interest Centers				

Figure 3.8. Blank differentiated curriculum planner.

Discipline	September	October	November	December
Science	Scientific Method	Simple Machines Unit		Life Cycles
Math	Numeration, Whole Numbers, Computation	→→→→→	Fractions	Geometry
Literature	Genre: Mystery	→→→→→	Genre: Fantasy	Genre: Biography
Communications	Narrative Writing	→→→→→		
Social Studies	North Carolina Resources, Geography/ Landforms	Products, Manufacturing	History	→→→→→
Interdisciplinary Units	Unsolved Mysteries		Invention Convention	Under Construction
Interest Centers	Clue, Nancy Drew/Hardy Boys Book Club; Red Herrings		Marble Works, Rube Goldberg	Tesselations, Line Designs, Bisecting Angles

Table title: Differentiated Curriuclum Planner — Grade Level:_____

Figure 3.9. Completed differentiated curriculum planner.

Lesson Modification Sheet			
Content	**Process**	**Product**	**Learning Environment**

Figure 3.10. Blank lesson modification sheet.

Lesson Modification Sheet			
Content	**Process**	**Product**	**Learning Environment**
• Basic Genealogy • Gods/Goddesses • Myths	• Compare myths • Compare and contrast versions of myths from different cultures	• Create an original genealogy • Write original myth • Create a song using vocabulary of mythology or discussing origins • Create an interview with a mythological character	• Students grouped by ability and interest • Technology advisor in computer room using internet • Media specialist in center • Props for dramatization in art class

Figure 3.11. Completed lesson modification sheet.

Gifted Education Specialist Planning Log

Theme:_____

Grade Level:_____   Date:_____

Teachers Involved: _____

_____

Agenda:_____

_____

_____

_____

_____

_____

_____

Accomplishments:_____

_____

_____

_____

_____

_____

_____

To Be Completed:_____

_____

_____

_____

_____

_____

Attach completed lesson plan when applicable.

Figure 3.12. Blank gifted education specialist planning log.

Gifted Education Specialist Planning Log

Theme: Systems

Grade Level: 4   Date: 1/20/00

Teachers Involved: all fourth-grade teachers

Agenda: • Get feedback on last lesson

         • Plan problem-solving project

         • Schedule times to check students' work folders

Accomplishments: • Lesson deemed successful, will repeat in future

         • Problem-solving project planned (create an original math graph)

To Be Completed: • Assign tasks for each teacher for problem-solving project

         • Schedule time to check student work folders next.

Attach completed lesson plan when applicable.

Figure 3.13. Completed gifted education specialist planning log (4th grade).

Gifted Education Specialist Planning Log

Theme: Relationships

Grade Level: 2   Date: 11/2/01

Teachers Involved: all second-grade teachers

Agenda: • Discussion centered around the "Aunt Sally" simulation

Accomplishments: • Students will receive the friendly letter stimulus for the "Aunt Sally" simulation this week. I will provide a creativity lesson and a geography lesson this week for the students involved (one classroom teacher will team teach with me).

• Classroom teachers will read two books orally to whole classes about trips and/ or destinations. I will provide travel materials and maps.

To Be Completed: • Next week the focus will be on the creative writing involved in the project (friendly letter and journal writing).

• Budgeting the trip will be the final stage. Classroom staff will provide work with calculators and estimation.

• Project evaluation will be conducted the week of May 24th.

Attach completed lesson plan when applicable.

Figure 3.14. Completed gifted education specialist planning log (2nd grade).

		Consultation and Collaboration Monthly Calendar		
Directions: Record frequency with hatch marks (each mark equals an incidence of 1).				
Type of Activity	**Target Participants**	**Resources Used**	**Time Involved**	**Other**
<u>Types of Lessons</u> ___Collaborative lesson ___Implement lesson ___Demonstration lesson ___Observation lesson ___Pull-out lesson ___Team-taught lesson	<u>Gifted Students Served</u> ___1-5 ___6-10 ___11-15 ___16-20 ___21-24 ___25+	<u>Types of Instructional Materials</u> ___Gifted program materials ___Personal materials ___Library materials ___Classroom materials ___Other general education materials ___Supplementary materials for use in regular classroom ___Other materials	<u>Time for Initial Contact</u> ___1-15 min. ___16-30 min. ___31-60 min. ___1-2 hrs. ___1/2 day ___full day	Comments:
<u>Instructional Materials Development</u> ___Pull-out materials ___Develop new materials ___Collect and desseminate materials	<u>Non-gifted Students Served</u> ___1-5 ___6-10 ___11-15 ___16-20 ___21-24 ___25+		<u>Planning Time</u> ___1-15 min. ___16-30 min. ___31-60 min. ___1-2 hrs. ___1/2 day ___full day	
<u>Student Identification</u> ___Assist in student assessment ___Attend eligibility meeting ___Conduct assessment	<u>No. of Teachers Involved in Collaboration</u> ___1 ___2-3 ___4+		<u>Time for Implementation</u> ___1-15 min. ___16-30 min. ___31-60 min. ___1-2 hrs. ___1/2 day ___full day	
<u>Conferences</u> ___Parent conference ___Student conference ___Teacher conference	<u>Types of Collaboration</u> ___by grade level ___one-on-one ___small group ___large group		<u>Time for Follow-up</u> ___1-15 min. ___16-30 min. ___31-60 min. ___1-2 hrs. ___1/2 day ___full day	

<u>Figure 3.15.</u> Blank monthly consultation and collaboration form.

Consultation and Collaboration Monthly Calendar				
Directions: Record frequency with hatch marks (each mark equals an incidence of 1).				
Type of Activity	**Target Participants**	**Resources Used**	**Time Involved**	**Other**

Types of Lessons
 	
//// Collaborative lesson
// Implement lesson
//// Demonstration lesson
// Observation lesson
___ Pull-out lesson
/// Team-taught lesson
	Gifted Students Served
	
	// 1-5
	/// 6-10
	/ 11-15
	/ 16-20
	___ 21-24
	/// 25+
		Types of Instructional Materials
		
		/// Gifted program materials
		/// Personal materials
		/// Library materials
		/// Classroom materials
		// Other general education materials
		/// Supplementary materials for use in regular classroom
		/ Other materials
			Time for Initial Contact
			
			/ 1-15 min.
			/ 16-30 min.
			/// 31-60 min.
			/ 1-2 hrs.
			___ 1/2 day
			/ full day
				Comments:
				
				Conducted curriculum mapping for third-grade math.
				
				Set up inservices for rest of school year.

Instructional Materials Development ___ Pull-out materials // Develop new materials /// Collect and desseminate materials	Non-gifted Students Served / 1-5 // 6-10 ___ 11-15 /// 16-20 ___ 21-24 / 25+		Planning Time // 1-15 min. // 16-30 min. ////// 31-60 min. / 1-2 hrs. ___ 1/2 day / full day	
Student Identification / Assist in student assessment / Attend eligibility meeting // Conduct assessment	No. of Teachers Involved in Collaboration / 1 //// 2-3 // 4+		Time for Implementation // 1-15 min. // 16-30 min. / 31-60 min. ___ 1-2 hrs. / 1/2 day / full day	
Conferences / Parent conference / Student conference / Teacher conference	Types of Collaboration // by grade level //// one-on-one / small group //// large group		Time for Follow-up / 1-15 min. // 16-30 min. /// 31-60 min. / 1-2 hrs. / 1/2 day / full day	

Figure 3.16. Completed monthly consultation and collaboration form.

Guidelines for Student Grouping

In a Resource Consultation and Collaboration Program, appropriate grouping not only enhances student instruction by providing a like-minded environment of peers with similar mental abilities, but it also helps the gifted education specialist manage the number of collegial relationships he or she must maintain. (Typically a ratio of 12-15 teachers per gifted education specialist at any one time is manageable.) While individual schools will find that some practices are more effective than others given their student population, facilities, and staff, underlying

any particular set of grouping practices should be a commitment to collaboratively developed pre-assessment policies and criteria that allow students to flow into and out of groups or classrooms as their educational needs dictate (see Figure 3.17). Following are guidelines for establishing and maintaining student groups for the dual purposes of providing effective instruction and assisting the gifted education specialists in maintaining a manageable schedule.

Grouping Criteria

- Pretest scores of at least 88%
- Reading level
- Past performance on proficiency tests
- Superior achievement test scores
- Accelerated classroom performance
- Advanced curriculum-based assessment outcomes
- Exemplary portfolio and product reviews

Figure 3.17. Sample criteria for grouping students.

1. Maintain clusters of 8-10 gifted learners in participating general education classrooms. Smaller groups of students spread across many classrooms present a logistical nightmare for specialists who must then work with too many teachers at any given time. Teachers also find that many of the best practices for intervention with this population of students work best with small groups rather than whole classrooms or individual students. For example, a Socratic seminar with one or two children is as unsucessful as it is with twenty, but it works well with a group of eight students.

2. Use team teaching in a way that allows a free-flow of target students into and out of instructional groupings. For example, if third-grade teachers decide to assess student achievement and overall readiness several times a year and group students according to similar levels, students can be placed into appropriate instructional groups as their needs change. While the gifted education teacher works with students from the general education classrooms who have demonstrated content mastery, the classroom teacher has a chance to work with the students remaining in the classroom at their level and at a pace commensurate with their learning needs.

3. Create individual and small groups of gifted learners for pull-out sessions with the gifted education specialist. Teachers from the same or different grade levels can group students according to advanced ability, achievement, learning style, and/or interest levels. The gifted education specialist can then work with this unique group of students in separate small groups or all at once on differentiated learning that is an extension of the core curricula.

4. Divide groups of students for instructional activities based on a commonly agreed upon rubric. The gifted education specialist and classroom teachers should pre-assess and divide a classroom of students into subgroups using a differentiated rubric commonly agreed upon by all of the educators during the planning phase.

5. Allow students to "test out" of whole classroom instruction so that they can work on differentiated learning activities. Before conducting whole-group lessons, classroom teachers should pre-assess students and allow them to work on alternate instructional activities developed collaboratively with the gifted education specialist. These activities can take place in the classroom or in another location under the direction of the specialist.

6. Create homogenous ability groups for instruction following whole-group introductory lessons and preceding whole-group culminating activities. Often the best time to group students by ability level and needs is during the mastery development period of an instructional unit. Gifted learners bring more existing knowledge to a unit of study as well as learn brand new material at an accelerated rate compared to their same age peers. As a result, gifted learners often need fewer, if any, drill and mastery development activities following the initial introduction of new material. While other students are involved in these mastery activities, gifted students should receive differentiated activities that allow them to delve into a topic more deeply or extend their learning beyond what the regular curriculum allows.

7. Develop multi-age classrooms with gifted learners. Collaboration is most effective when students are grouped by ability and interest, and one way of accommodating students with common learning needs is by establishing a multi-age grouping of students for specific subjects (e.g., math or reading) or in homeroom. The gifted education specialist works with the teacher to provide differentiated instruction and activities matched to the mental-age and interests of the cross-age group of students.

8. Establish self-contained classrooms of students with similar needs, especially gifted learners with advanced learning needs. Best practices for differentiated instruction are applied most successfully when gifted learners are taught in moderate numbers rather than with the one or two typically placed in a heterogeneous classroom. Further, homogeneous grouping is important for the cognitive and social-emotional development of gifted learners. When practicing collaboration, this grouping strategy facilitates co-planning, co-teaching, and follow-up because it allows the gifted education specialist to focus on only a few classrooms.

9. Move students from one collaboration classroom to another at a higher grade-level for partial or full acceleration. When students are accelerated from one traditional classroom to another, no differentiation necessarily occurs. However, when stu-

dents are moved from one cluster group to another at an advanced grade level, the gifted education specialist and the classroom teacher can differentiate instruction based on advanced students' needs.

10. Move students through stations or interest centers with differentiated activities. At the direction of the classroom teacher, students can move through specific stations or through all stations. The classroom teachers and gifted education specialist can work together to plan, implement, and evaluate student performance, though typically the gifted education specialist monitors the progress of gifted and other high-end learners.

11. Trade students among teachers in the same or different grade-level classrooms to create groups for differentiated instruction. Teachers at the same or different grade levels can assess student readiness and group students across their classrooms. This flexible grouping minimizes the number of different levels of learning opportunities that any individual teacher must develop, and the gifted education specialist can focus on the classrooms with high-end learners. Because the gifted education specialist works with a group of students, this type of grouping reduces the number of students needing direct instruction in the classroom and improves the teacher-to-student ratio during instructional delivery.

Guidelines for Student Assessment

Appropriately assessing student performance is an important aspect of gifted education. Typically, educators assess gifted learners' outcomes using grade-level standards rather than a notion of continuous progress. Because many gifted learners have pre-existing knowledge of content and are able to understand the content at levels beyond other students at their chronological age level, age-appropriate student assessments often lower the achievement standards for high-ability learners. Therefore, as educators modify instructional activities, they must also change the assessment approaches so that feedback accurately reflects student learning and progress.

In a Resource Consultation and Collaboration Program, classroom teachers and gifted education specialists work together to modify assessment tools to take into account varying student abilities. The modifications can be as simple as adapting traditional evaluation measures, such as classroom tests, to reflect more in-depth learning. For example, the classroom teacher and gifted education specialist can develop separate items for a test or modify existing items. Educators can also work together to develop differentiated work product rubrics that reflect varying ability levels. Additionally, the gifted education specialist can set up and manage student portfolios (e.g., process and product folders), which he or she can periodically assess. Because gifted learners' differentiated learning activities replace regular education assignments, grades on these assignments are incorporated into regular student grades, and grades, then, reflect continual progress in learning rather than an evaluation of previously learned material.

Evaluation Rubrics

Each of the alternative assessment strategies involves rubrics or evaluation criteria in some form. All assessment practices should reflect standards of performance commensurate with gifted learners' advanced abilities. The teacher and gifted education specialist develop rubrics or frameworks together prior to initiating the activity, and students should receive these rubrics or criteria at the beginning of the assignment so that they know what is expected of them. Rubrics may contain a rating scale that reflects the level or degree of performance, and feedback should relate directly to the criteria for performance established at the beginning of the activity. Several examples of rubrics for assessing student learning follow in Figure 3.18.

Sample Evaluation Rubrics

Example 1

Generic Rubric for Evaluating Project

Criteria:

_____

_____

_____

_____

_____

Performance Level:

4=exceeds expectations
3=meets expectations
2=partially meets expectations
1=needs immediate improvement

Example 2

Rubric for Myths Independent Study

1. Contains all components.
   a. Complete collection of myths and visuals
   b. Timeline
   c. World map and locations plotted
   d. Own myth and visual
   e. Proved generalization

2. Includes complete and thorough research.

3. Presents an organized and complete oral report..
   a. Used visuals at appropriate time
   b. Confident and poised when speaking

4. Comes prepared to work sessions.

Figure 3.18. Sample evaluation rubrics.

Example 3

Project Rubric for Probability Game

Requirements:

Overall Design (be original; don't copy an existing game)

Time Limit (the winner must be determined within a thirty-minute limit)

Directions (develop clear directions)

Materials (include all that are needed)

Challenge (make the game fun and interesting; involve probability)

Mechanics (eliminate spelling, punctuation, and capitalization errors)

Neatness (make attractive; print/type directions; use a ruler for drawing)

Creativity (develop game around a topic or theme)

Example 4

Weekly Rubric for Hawk Research Project

Name:_____ **Date:**_____

Directions: Complete this self-evaluation rubric each week by filling in the date and rating your behavior.

_____**I learn well.**

_____**I think about information.**

_____**I use information to solve problems.**   **Performance Level Rating Scale:**

_____**I understand big ideas.**

_____**I consistently solve problems.**   4=WOW!
3=I meet the challenge
_____**I make careful decisions based on facts.**   2=I can do better.
1=I must do better.
_____**I make sensible decisions based on facts.**

_____**My product creatively shows what I've learned.**

_____**My product connects with big ideas.**

_____**I used a variety of resources to make my product.**

_____**I stay focused on my tasks when working independently.**

_____**I stay focused on my tasks when working with my group.**

_____**I work well with others.**

_____**I am willing to participate.**

_____**I consistently complete my work on time.**

Teacher/Student Comments:

_____

_____

_____

_____

Figure 3.18. Sample evaluation rubrics (cont.).

Example 5

Animal Slideshow Rubric

Criteria:	Student Rating	Teacher Rating
Includes animal riddle, student's name.		
Labels habitat on map.		
Includes accurate diet of animal.		
Uses research to describe structure of animal.		
Includes accurate picture of animal in the wild.		
States a big idea about the animal.		
Includes voice narration for slideshow.		
Understands and uses slideshow independently		

Rating Scale:

4=Outstanding   3=Very Good   2=Satisfactory   1=Needs Improvement

Example 4

Project Rubric

Criteria:	Rating Scale:
On Time	1=below standard; not acceptable
Oral Presentation	2=adequate effort; some missing pieces
Knowledge	3=meets requirements; complete; neat
Creativity	4=superior; above expectations
Thoroughness	

Figure 3.18. Sample evaluation rubrics (cont.).

Self-Evaluation

The gifted education specialist often takes the lead in preparing and implementing differentiated learning experiences, but he or she rarely sees students on a daily basis. Therefore, teaching students how to evaluate and report on their products and progress becomes an important part of the assessment process. Educators can develop rating scales or prompts to stimulate and guide students' higher-level thinking and documentation of the thought processes, and students can record meta-cognitive processing (how students think about their thinking) and reflections in journals that the gifted education specialist monitors. Not only does self-evaluation help the specialist monitor learning, but it helps students build skills for being lifelong learners.

Developing Supportive Environments

Consultation and collaboration practices thrive in supportive and nurturing environments, and what teachers believe and act on about themselves and students is a large part of that environment. For resource consultation and collaboration to work, every educator involved must let go of complete control over the classroom and learn to share that control. As educators open up their classrooms to other people's input, they accept a shared responsibility for teaching gifted learners. Each educator involved in the program must believe that the gifted learners' needs are a priority for everyone involved in their education. It follows, then, that all educators must have a mutual respect for one another demonstrated by an acceptance of and appreciation for one another's competencies in planning, implementing, and assessing differentiated learning experiences. Without this mutual respect, the give and take that leads to mutual agreement over a common plan for providing appropriate differentiated services—the heart of the consultation and collaboration process—will not occur.

To promote that respect, program leadership must articulate that each teacher's role in the consultation and collaborative processes is essential for overall program success, and teachers must be confident in their unique roles in the collaborative process. One of the most vital aspects of the learning environment is individual teachers' understanding of their roles in planning, implementing, and evaluating students' learning experiences. Without an understanding of where he or she fits into the overall process, a teacher may not perform his or her responsibilities according to plans laid out in planning sessions. Those who are leaders in the program should monitor participation and support inservice activities to help teachers develop confidence in their roles in the program.

In addition, several beliefs about the roles of students in the learning environment are requisite to the success of collaboration and consultation. First, children must be allowed to flow into and out of the classroom and other learning environments. One of the many benefits of collaboration is that multiple learning environments are accessible with more than one person directing learning. It is sometimes most efficient to have students move to environments that provide resources commensurate with the level of their learning. For example, students may need to attend other classroom lessons on a part-time basis to participate in learning experiences appropriate to their needs. Likewise, some students may need to spend time in small groups at interest centers in the back of the classroom to work on differentiated activities. The physical environment of the school must permit students to move around the general education classroom and allow for independent and small-group work. In short, all participants must be accepting of all possible environments for matching needs to differentiated learning, and teachers must be willing to accept the movement of students within and outside the classroom to facilitate the use of best instructional practices for high ability learners.

Scheduling

Without a doubt, two of the most difficult tasks within a Resource Consultation and Collaboration Program are developing and maintaining a suitable schedule for activities. There are two types of schedules: those that are flexible and those that are more stable. The nature of student grouping, the overall school schedule, and the number of days a gifted education specialist spends in any given school are all factors that affect the flexibility of the schedule. A more flexible schedule allows for more spontaneous development of differentiation, but it can also become chaotic and overwhelming. Ultimately, a good schedule is a compromise between the two extremes: it will be flexible enough to accommodate the various needs of staff and students in the building and spontaneous requests for collaboration, but it will also have established times set aside for long-term and short-term planning and a balance among direct and indirect services for which teachers and gifted educational specialists are responsible. Figure 3.19 displays two sample work schedules of gifted education specialists in a Resource Consultation and Collaboration Program.

As program administrators build a schedule for resource consultation and collaboration activities, they must keep a number of considerations in mind. First, participants must have a dependable 30-45-minute block of weekly planning time for each grade level or subject area. Regular meetings allow educators to establish a continuous dialogue and maintain collaboration efforts over time. Another scheduling concern surrounds the total time the gifted education specialist spends in co-planning with teachers. The amount of time that any single gifted education specialist spends in planning can drastically reduce instructional time. One strategy for managing the time the specialist spends in planning with colleagues is to limit the overall number of classroom clusters of students and thus the number of teachers who participate in the collaborative process. For example, the specialist could work with two classrooms that each have a cluster of eight to ten high-ability learners rather than four classrooms with four or five gifted learners each. Further, a school might target priority need areas (e.g., literacy or math) and block time in the schedule for the gifted education specialist to work with students and teachers during these times. Prioritizing subject areas or disciplines for which the gifted education specialist is responsible minimizes the number of overall preparations that any one specialist has across grade levels. Finally, the school staff can appeal to administrators to work with overall school schedules to prevent scheduling conflicts (e.g., to prevent grade level or department planning times from occurring at the same time as collaboration and consultation planning times).

Program Evaluation

Accountability for program effectiveness is critical to the initial acceptance of the program and its durability. Accountability comes from assurances that programming is effective, which is best determined by program evaluation. Both formative and summative evaluations are critical parts of the overall program assessment. To evaluate a program appropriately, participants must

Example 1:

Time	Day One	Day Two
8:45-9:30 a.m.	Fifth-grade math (pull-out)	Fifth-grade math (collaborative lesson)
9:40-10:40 a.m.	Third-grade math	Individual student (third grader for math)
10:45-11:45 a.m.	Second-grade problem solving	Lunch and planning
11:45 a.m.-12:45 p.m.	Lunch and planning	Fourth-grade math
12:45-1:45 p.m.	Fourth-grade literacy	Fourth-grade literacy
2:00-3:00 p.m.	Fifth-grade literacy	Fifth-grade literacy

Example 2:

Day One

Parent meeting
Math lab (individual student work)
Grade-level planning
Student research lesson
Evaluation of student products
Cooperative teaching
Lesson preparation

Day Two

Cooperative teaching lesson
Pull-out group of students
Grade-level planning
Grade-level planning
Student identification
Math group
Lesson preparation

Day Three

Reading group
Lesson preparation
Science fair group
Math lab (individual student work)
Evaluation of student work products
Pull-out group of students

Day Four

Math group
Student research lesson
Demonstration lesson
Grade-level planning
Weekly book club
Lesson preparation

Day Five

Reading group
Science fair group
Develop learning center
Pull-out group of students
Grade-level planning
Cooperative teaching lesson

Figure 3.19. Sample schedules for gifted education specialists.

collect data that reflects the overall effectiveness of the program as well as the desired program outcomes and successful operations, best practices, and the use of personnel, resource, and materials.

Generally the gifted education specialist collects data regarding the activities of a Resource Consultation and Collaboration Program and records the information by frequency on monthly calendars (see Figure 3.16). To keep track of student performance data from differentiated lessons, the specialist also typically maintains confidential files on achievement assessment data for students that demonstrate ability. The gifted education specialist should also collect data on instructional practices and teacher behavior, including change in teacher competencies and knowledge-base. He or she should record the benefits to target students and the spillover effects to the entire school.

The classroom teacher also keeps records related to the Resource Consultation and Collaboration Program, such as activities that do not include the gifted education specialist and student pre-assessment information. Classroom teachers and/or the gifted education specialist might assign grades on students' work products during differentiated lessons, but the classroom teacher usually maintains these records.

During the initial stages of program development, both classroom teachers and gifted education specialists should keep personal journals on their reflections about the program. Educators then share these thoughts anonymously with program administrators and/or evaluators so that administrators can tailor the program to individual teacher and school needs.

One of the most comprehensive records of resource consultation and collaboration processes is the consultation log or journal. Figure 3.20 illustrates specific items that are typically documented in a consultation log or journal. A log is a written record of consultation and collaboration activities. A journal, on the other hand, is an interactive record that allows for feedback and reflection by the author and others and requires more reflection. Whether a school keeps a consultation log or journal is up to the individual school staff, although most schools currently employing a Resource Consultation and Collaboration Program keep logs. They do not take as much time to create and maintain as they are simply records of activities that have occurred. Nonetheless, in many of these programs, individual teachers chose to maintain their own personal program journals in which they reflected on activities that had occurred in their classroom and of which they had been a part.

Program Log or Journal

• Informal, spontaneous meetings
• Planned meetings
• Problem-solving meetings
• Phone calls
• Follow-through activities related to meetings
• Observations of student behavior
• Planning Sessions
• Frequency of direct or indirect services

Figure 3.20. Information to include in program log or journal.

Some additional documentation for program goals include:

- Portfolios of program efforts (e.g., process and product folios)

- Records of student achievement
- Student performance reports (e.g., grades)
- Student work product assessment
- Entries in consultation log and/or journal
- Records of program activity
- Observation of teacher performance
- Staff interviews

Regardless of the program format, all gifted education programming efforts should be evaluated rigorously on an on-going basis. The gifted education specialist should evaluate program effectiveness and its potential to grow and evolve into a more productive and efficient program. In analyzing all of the data that participants have gathered, the gifted education specialist should also look for information that can lead to program enhancement and refinement.

Program Activities Timeline

Although each Resource Consultation and Collaboration Program is unique, schools must move through specific steps to develop a successful program. These steps represent *minimum* program activities or outcomes during a two-year timeframe. Most schools take two years to develop and implement the program (Landrum, 2001), and schools can measure their progress toward the program's full implementation by successfully completing the benchmark program activities outlined in the timeline in Figure 3.21. These benchmark program activities serve first as guideposts by defining tasks and designating places along a continuum of program implementation. Parents and other constituency groups can measure program development by comparing program efforts with the timeline. As the program progresses, these guideposts can become part of program evaluation as the school, parents, and others assess whether and to what degree each benchmark program activity is achieved. Therefore, what start as guideposts for program development and implementation soon become indices of program evaluation.

Developing and implementing a Resource Consultation and Collaboration program requires a long-term commitment. Though progress may seem slow at first, schools that carefully and deliberately consider each aspect of program development—scheduling, grouping, documentation, planning, environments—will develop a strong foundation on which the program, students, and teachers can flourish.

Program Timeline

Year One
- Conduct introductory inservice on overview of the model.
- Communicate role of the gifted education specialist to classroom teachers.
- Establish minimum weekly planning time with all classroom teachers.
- Establish minimum number of cluster-groups of gifted learners at each grade level.
- Conduct inservice training on the collaboration model and process.
- Inform parents of implementation of the program.
- Develop collaborative relationships among staff.
- Gifted education specialist develops short-term schedule or calendar.
- Gifted education specialist develops long-term schedule or calendar.
- Record/document all collaborative and consultative efforts on a universally accepted planner.
- Conduct minimum long-term planning for classroom instruction with classroom teachers.
- Establish types of indirect and direct services that the gifted specialist will provide.
- Gifted education specialist conducts demonstration lessons.
- Gifted education specialist conducts general education observation lessons,
- Gifted education specialist and general education teachers engage in cooperative teaching.
- Gifted education specialist and classroom general education teachers pretest students to determine flexible student group status for participation in collaborative lessons.
- Gifted education specialist and classroom general education teachers collaboratively evaluate student performance.

Year Two
- Develop permanent procedures for recording/documenting collaborative and consultative efforts.
- Refine program management techniques.
- Create a balance between indirect and direct services.
- Create a balance of collaborative effort and participation between classroom and gifted education specialists.
- Conduct inservice training on differentiation.
- Classroom teachers and gifted education specialist establish supplementary curricula materials for gifted learners in the general education classroom.
- Classroom teachers adopt new instructional practices.
- Gifted education specialist conducts a minimal number of demonstration and observation lessons.

Ongoing Tasks
- Gifted education specialist maintains weekly planning time with all general education teachers who have clusters of gifted students.
- Gifted education specialist maintains a minimum number of cluster-groups of gifted learners established at each grade level.
- Gifted education specialist and classroom teachers pretest students to determine flexible student group status for participation in collaborative lessons.
- Gifted education specialist and classroom teachers collaboratively evaluate student performance.
- Gifted education specialist continues long-term planning for differentiated classroom instruction with classroom teachers.
- Develop on-going strategies for informing parents of implementation and development of the program.

Figure 3.21. Program timeline.

Staff Development in Resource Consultation & Collaboration Programs

"What is best about teaching this way is that you always have someone to go to for support or assistance. It's a true team effort" —Classroom Teacher

Just as students (including the brightest students) need guidance and training to learn what is expected of them and how to do it, so do educators. If schools instating a Resource Consultation and Collaboration Program do not clearly articulate or provide training for the roles and responsibilities of each staff member, the program will fail. Administrators must make deliberate efforts to ensure that all staff involved in the program understand where and how they fit into the program. In addition, administrators must provide educators with ongoing training in resource consultation and collaboration objectives and methodology as well as incentives to attend and make the most of training sessions.

Program Staff Roles

Many people with diverse roles are involved in the resource consultation process, each lending his or her expertise to the educational program. Although unique combinations of educators characterize individual Resource Consultation and Collaboration Programs, outlined below are the most common roles the program.

Classroom Teachers: Classroom teachers are the most essential components of the Resource Consultation and Collaboration Program in gifted education. Every teacher who has gifted learners in his or her classroom must work collaboratively with gifted education specialists to plan, deliver, and assess differentiated educational experiences for target students as frequently as necessary.

Gifted Education Specialists: The gifted education specialist maintains the core role in Resource Consultation and Collaboration programs in gifted education, delivering both direct and indirect services. Without the specialist, the differentiated nature of learning experiences that evolve from the program are severely limited in quality and quantity. A ratio of one gifted education specialist to twelve teachers is recommended. While one specialist may serve more than one school in a district, more than two schools per specialist can adversely affect the frequency and duration of direct services. At the middle school level, greater numbers of students and the demands of mastering a variety of content areas limit direct services across all content areas. To preserve time for direct services, two gifted education specialists per school are recommended at the middle school level.

Supporting Staff: Other educators such as media specialists and technology coordinators often join the classroom teacher and gifted education specialist in providing differentiated lessons to target students. As the program develops, support staff and classroom teachers may repeat activities that initially involved the gifted education specialist or develop differentiated learning opportunities for gifted learners without the specialist. For example, early in the program, a classroom teacher, gifted education specialist, and media specialist may work together to develop differentiated research lessons for gifted learners. Over time, the classroom teacher and the media specialist might implement these lessons without the gifted specialist.

Program Consultant: The program consultant is an outside expert in resource consultation and collaboration practices. This person helps schools get started and can serve in an advisory role as the program develops. He or she can also help direct staff development activities for the school. Schools that need to locate a consultant to help with their programs may be able to get advice and suggestions from those in school psychology or special education, as the model finds its roots in these areas.

Building Administrators: Though their role may not involve direct content with students, building and district-level school administrators are vital parts of the collaborative process. Administrators must institute flexible grouping practices for students and help teachers and the gifted education specialist balance schedules. In particular, ensuring that educators have regular instructional planning sessions and clustering gifted students within a few classrooms (as opposed to having only one or two gifted learners in every classroom) are crucial to the resource consultation process. In addition, administrators may be called upon to sanction alternative service delivery options such as partial or full acceleration.

Gifted Program Administrator: The gifted program administrator is that person in charge of gifted education programming in the building or school district. This person will be very involved in managing the logistics of the program, such as staff development and scheduling.

Parents: Interested parents can play important support roles in a Resource Consultation and Collaboration Program. Parents can help develop, implement, or evaluate differentiated lessons; bring their own expertise to the instructional setting by giving presentations; serve as mentors; lead sessions developed by someone else; stand in as substitutes so that teachers can attend planning or inservice sessions; and much more. For example, a parent could lead book discussions, help collect instructional resources for classroom teachers who will lead differentiated lessons, or work with an individual student doing an independent study based on a common interest.

Staff Training for Collaboration and Consultation

Many professional educators have not had formal training in how resource consultation and collaboration works. Program administrators must provide educators with training to develop effective and efficient consultation and collaboration skills. The staff development program should provide participants with the information they need to build an understanding of resource consultation and collaboration, grounding in methodologies for collaboration and differentiation, and a vision toward which all participants are working—meeting the educational needs of students. While building a knowledge base in gifted education and learning how to recognize gifted behaviors are important parts of teacher training, differentiated curricula and instruction are at the root of services provided in a Resource Consultation and Collaboration Program; teaching educators the tools and techniques for providing these services is, therefore, a critical part of staff development.

Training sessions should also offer educators a chance to share information with one another, validate and reinforce emerging successes, and provide critical feedback for further growth and development. Overall, staff training should serve to motivate educators, urging them to continue to develop and refine their skills and forge professional relationships that will help them provide appropriate educational experiences to students.

Training Level of Participants

Important parts of any Resource Consultation and Collaboration Program are its participants' unique talents and competencies. However, each participant fulfilling a role in the program needs to come to the program with a certain base level of knowledge.

Gifted Education Specialist: The gifted education specialist is the expert in gifted education and must possess a comprehensive, current knowledgebase and competency in this area. In particular, this person must possess knowledge of the nature and needs of gifted learners and competency in appropriate curriculum differentiation best practices. It is not necessary that he or she have taught before, but it does increase the validity of the consulting role.

Classroom Teachers: The classroom teacher must be an expert in the content that is taught at his or her grade level and must have a current and diverse knowledge of instructional practices. An understanding of or appreciation for the need to individualize education for all learners enhances the resource consultation process.

Support Personnel: Each support personnel brought into the collaboration process must have a current and diverse knowledge base in his or her area of expertise. This person must have an appropriate command of the variety of instructional practices that promote student learning.

Building/School Administrators: Administrators involved in the program must possess strong leadership skills. The ability to manage school programs efficiently and direct educational reform and change are important. A desire to serve and reach all children is not necessarily required, but it is very helpful.

Parents: Schools should inform parents about the nature of the Resource Consultation and Collaboration Program in gifted education and the benefits it has to their children and all children served by the school. Any expertise that parents have can be channeled into program efforts. A desire to advocate for high ability children in positive ways and work with the school are the most desirable traits of program parents.

Staff Development

The staff development model for collaboration and consultation is hierarchical and builds on a strong initial inservice session. Follow-up inservice sessions should become increasingly more sophisticated and specific in nature. The staff development plan should focus on three levels: a general overview of resource consultation and collaboration, best practices in curriculum differentiation, and an advanced curriculum differentiation strand. Any number of inservice sessions on various topics can transpire at each level of the model depending upon the needs and interests of target participants. Figure 4.1 highlights the major focus of each level of the staff development model and denotes several sample inservice session topics.

Initial Inservice Content

An initial inservice workshop scheduled at the beginning of developing a Resource Consultation and Collaboration program is absolutely critical to the success of the program. Very early in the program schedule, classroom teachers and gifted education specialists must come together for a one-day workshop. The first half of the inservice day should focus on an overview of the Resource Consultation and Collaboration Program (see Figure 4.2). The most important part of this morning session is to make sure all participants understand how the program will operate and what roles and responsibilities they will have in the program. Everyone should have a good sense of the components and mechanics of the program and a general

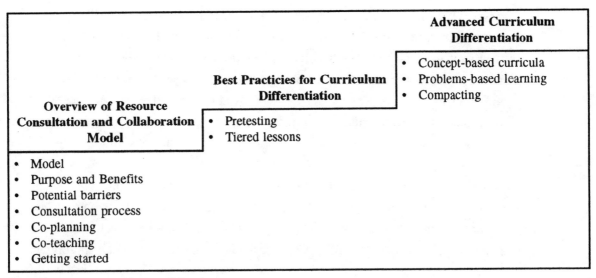

Figure 4.1. Three levels of staff development.

sense of their roles in the program. Support personnel and administrators can also attend this portion of the inservice.

The second half of the workshop involves a hands-on approach to collaborative differentiation practices. The inservice leaders should present best practices and sample lessons. During this session, small groups of teachers should have time to begin planning how to differentiate the curriculum and instruction. An overview of collaborative practices for differentiating curricula is also contained in Figure 4.2.

Overview of Resource Consultation and Collaboration in Gifted Education	Collaborative Practices for Differentiating Curricula for Gifted Learners
• Purpose, nature, and benefits of resource consultation in gifted education • Consultation and collaboration processes • Indirect and direct services • Cooperative teaching practices • Resource consultation program activities	• Compacting • Tiered lessons • Interest centers, contracts, and independent studies • Designing differentiated rubrics for gifted learners' work products

Figure 4.2. Inservice workshop content.

Staff Development Activities

In order to address the different needs of participants and also to best deliver the needed services, program leaders (the program consultant and/or the gifted education specialist) should employ a variety of staff development activities. The following activities have proven particularly effective for developing consultation and collaboration competencies:

Inservice Workshops: Half-day and full-day inservice sessions should provide specific content on the nature of gifted child education and consultation and collaboration processes. Typically all staff across schools join together to participate. These sessions should be spread across the school year to give participants time to reflect and implement strategies and ideas. While these sessions are important, they can be kept to a minimum: at least one half-day in the beginning of the year and one half-day in the middle of the year (approximately 2-3 months after the first session). Occasionally individual school staffs can meet for inservice sessions focused on the specific aspects of the Resource Consultation and Collaboration Program in their building.

Planning Sessions: Four times a year each participating school should conduct half- or full-day long-term planning sessions. Typically, grade level staff members work together while the gifted education specialist moves from meeting to meeting. Other staff members (e.g., media specialist, counselor) can join the sessions when appropriate.

Field Observations: The program consultant should visit schools and observe the staff at work. While shadowing the gifted education specialist, the program consultant can interact with all participants in the Resource Consultation and Collaboration Program and see how they work together. These observations allow program consultants to give the staff constructive feedback on their efforts. In addition, the consultant may participate in problem-solving sessions, watch collaboration lessons, meet with administrators, and talk with parents.

Newsletters: At the end of each field observation visit, the program consultant or gifted education specialist should construct a newsletter to distribute to the staffs in the Resource Consultation and Collaboration Program. The content of the newsletters should consist of observations, exemplary practices, new information regarding further development, resource lists, etc. The archived newsletters can be very useful to new schools that need guidance.

Site Visits: Staff members in participating schools should visit one another to gain insight into specific applications of the resource consultation and collaboration processes. Educators and other staff members can see firsthand how the program is working at another site. These visits are particularly useful when a school beginning a program visits a site that has been operating for a longer period of time. Visits can occur from one grade level to another, one discipline to another, or gifted education specialist to gifted education specialist.

Sharing Sessions: Staffs across schools can come together to share specific activities, lessons, projects, and materials used during resource consultation and collaboration. This meeting usually occurs once a year for a half- or full-day session. The program consultant, program administrator, or gifted education specialist should advertise these "share fairs" in advance to give every participant an opportunity to find something to share at the meeting.

Mentoring: During site visits, planning sessions or sharing sessions, project participants may find mentors in other staff members at schools already using the processes of consultation and collaboration. Teachers can meet for discussions, make site visits, and "shadow" a teacher for a day to gain insight into his or her work and role in the program. Over time, some staff members will emerge as leaders and can serve as mentors in a "trainer of teachers" model for developing the program in new schools.

Handbook: Program participants can develop a handbook for new staff and additional schools that join in district-wide efforts to develop Resource Consultation and Collaboration Programs. This handbook is a work in progress, and a three-ring binder allows staff to add resources and examples of exemplary practice.

Consultation Log or Journal: The gifted education specialist (as well as other staff) should keep a record of the resource consultation and collaboration efforts in his or her school. This record helps keep participants accountable and can help educators look back on activities and analyze their effectiveness. The consultation log or journal can become interactive, with peers, mentors, consultants, and others reflecting and responding about their work. From time to time, the program consultant should review these logs and provide feedback about efforts.

Staff Development Hints and Helpers

Staff development is a long-term process. Figure 4.3 contains a list of resources that can be useful for developing Resource Consultation and Collaboration Programs in gifted education. In addition, the following pointers may help program leaders guide and facilitate the process during the course of its evolution.

- Get administrators involved. It is very important that they endorse and support the staff development activities. They should also provide incentives for and praise attendance at inservice sessions. Their most important contribution to the process would be to attend sessions themselves. Not only does attendance at training sessions communicate their importance, but administrators also learn enough about the program to support the staff's efforts appropriately.
- Start the training process with everyone together; then target specific groups with more specialized training content. It is important to the success of the programming that every staff member in the school understand the fundamental elements of the Resource Consultation and Collaboration Model, including the purpose, goals, benefits, roles of all participants, and expected outcomes. Later more specialized training such as specific support for counselors or more advanced training in dif-

ferentiation for classroom teachers can become a part of inservice sessions.

- Employ a variety of staff development activities to address the diverse needs of the educational staff. As the staff development program evolves, conduct informal and formal needs assessments so that participants can adapt and modify plans to the specific needs of particular staff members.

- Provide viable incentives for staff development participation. Most participants in consultation and collaboration continue with the program because it serves specific needs. However, initial training and introduction to the program may require different incentives. Providing staff members with release time to attend training or resources to implement collaborative activities is important.

The clear articulation of the roles and responsibilities of each participating school staff member is vital to the success of a Resource Consultation and Collaboration Program. Likewise, introductory training helps educators build up skills in consultation and collaboration processes, making the process easier to manage and more efficient. However, on-going supportive training activities may offer the most to a program, as these activities allow teachers to forge relationships, reflect on activities, learn from mistakes, analyze other programs, and offer their own suggestions and ideas to larger groups. These staff development sessions and activities not only help educators develop competencies in resource consultation and collaboration processes, but they allow educators a chance to have a personal, creative stake in the program.

Resources for Staff Development Program Preparation

- Dettmer, P., Thurston, L. P., & Dyck, N. (1999). *Consultation, collaboration, and teamwork for students with special needs* (second edition). Needham Heights, MA: Allyn & Bacon.
- Dettmer, P. , and Landrum, M. S. (Eds.). (1998). *Staff development: The key to effective gifted education programs.* Waco, TX: Prufrock Press.
- Kirschenbaum, R., Armstrong, D. C., and Landrum, M. S. (1999). Resource consultation model in gifted education to support talent development in today's inclusive schools. *Gifted Child Quarterly,* 43(1), 39-47.
- Maker, C. J. (1993). *Critical issues in gifted education: Programs for the gifted in regular classrooms.* Austin, TX: Pro-Ed.
- Tomlinson, C. A. (1995). *How to differentiate instruction in mixed-ability classrooms.* Alexandria, VA: ASCD.
- Ward, S. B., & Landrum, M. S. (1994). Resource consultation: An alternative service delivery model for gifted education. *Gifted Child Quarterly,* 16(4), 272-279.

Figure 4.3. Inservice development resources.

Exemplary Practices in Differentiating Curricula and Instruction for Gifted Learners Through Resource Consultation & Collaboration

*"Gifted learners spend more time in the regular classroom than anywhere else.
That environment must be made conducive to gifted learners."—Program Consultant*

There are a number of goals educators must strive toward to meet the needs of gifted learners: continual student progress, advanced pace of learning, complexity of learning, and in-depth learning. In a Resource Consultation and Collaboration Program, the gifted education specialist must work together with classroom teachers to plan and deliver appropriately differentiated instruction that includes the in-depth study of complex and sophisticated content and encourages students to develop products that reflect their abilities and apply complex thinking and questioning as they are able.

Differentiated Instructional Practices

A differentiated learning experience occurs when educators modify the regular curriculum and select instructional practices that reflect students' readiness for learning. This "readiness" includes ability levels, achievement levels, interests, and learning preferences. To plan for differentiated learning, teachers must expand their view of the curriculum so that it can address the various levels of readiness of target students. The curriculum modification process includes making changes in all aspects of the curriculum, including content, process, and product.

Content Differentiation

Content refers to the knowledge, skills, attitudes, principles, ideas, concepts, and problems that educators present to students. Content modifications change the level of learning in the classroom for gifted learners by elevating the sophistication and complexity of what educators want students to know. Content modifications can remain integrated with the existing curriculum or become a part of newly developed or supplemental curricula.

Concept-based curriculum promotes the integration of key ideas, issues, and problems and easily accommodates content differentiation for high-end learning. Designated concepts or themes guide curriculum modifications: while regular classroom students study a particular topic at grade level, educators modify activities so that high-ability students develop a deeper understanding of the same concept. The collaborative process allows the classroom teacher to rely on the gifted education specialist to modify and adapt the core curriculum by integrating complex problems, issues, and ideas into the regular curriculum. For example, in lessons that focus on the universal concept of patterns, both average and high-ability students may study World War II and read *The Diary of a Young Girl: Anne Frank*. While average-ability students learn to recognize patterns in historical accuracies in historical and nonfiction accounts, advanced learners use the universal concept of patterns to enhance and extend their learning in an activity in which they predict the future of the Middle East given existing patterns of violence and war. Educators have taken a concept that is the focus of a particular unit (patterns) and modified activities so that gifted learners explore the complexity of the concept while average-ability students focus on the base concept. Using common concepts and themes for differentiating curricula also facilitates the transfer of learning from one classroom to another and supplies low and average learners with a larger context in which to place the ideas and materials they are studying.

Another strategy for differentiating content for gifted learners is to develop multi- and interdisciplinary courses of study that make connections among various subject areas. In any school setting this type of curriculum planning and maintenance is challenging, but in a collaborative school, the gifted education specialist can lead curriculum development sessions with classroom teachers to adapt and modify the core curriculum. The gifted education specialist and classroom teachers compact the general education curricula in two or more subjects, and during the "bought out" time, the gifted education specialist and classroom teacher co-teach lessons that complement and connect the compacted subject areas. For example, if a classroom teacher is teaching geometry and recycling to fifth-grade students at the same time, the gifted education specialist can construct a unit on tessellations. The lessons and activities guide students through a recycling project focused on making geometric designs out of plastic beverage rings.

Process Differentiation

Process refers to a student's mental processing of content, or what the student uses to "make sense of" content (Tomlinson, 1995). Process modifications for gifted learners address the advanced cognitive ability of gifted learners in terms of critical and creative thinking and provide a level of challenge that will encourage continuous growth for these students.

When addressing the needs of advanced learners, the most common problem with typical general classroom curricula is that it lacks the higher-order thinking needed to challenge these students. Infusing higher-order thinking skills into meaningful content within a discipline is a viable strategy for differentiating the curriculum for gifted learners. In a collaborative approach, the gifted education specialist can build students' skills in higher order thinking by teaching an entire program of thinking skills that can be infused in any content area. Classroom teachers can then differentiate any learning activity by elevating the level of thinking required of advanced learners.

In addition to infusing higher-order thinking skills into advanced content, educators can use higher order questioning to elevate students' processing. Using higher-level questioning in class discussions, on tests, and as part of student assignments gives students opportunities to process curriculum at a level commensurate with their advanced abilities. In a collaborative model the gifted education specialist modifies or adapts the regular curriculum by infusing higher level questioning into the learning experience or by adapting existing questions. For example, a fifth-grade classroom teacher doing a social studies lesson on economics can divide students into small groups based on ability. Instead of five questions of varying levels that most of the class receives, the advanced groups work on three higher-order questions that the gifted education specialist has prepared.

Another process strategy for differentiating learning experiences for gifted learners is integrating problem-solving skills into the curriculum. The gifted education specialist can introduce students to heuristics for problem solving so that students learn to identify and solve ill-structured and structured problems representative of real-world issues. The problems become the central focus of the content, with problem resolution becoming the primary process skill students use. Once students learn the necessary skills under the gifted education specialist's guidance, classroom teachers can infuse these skills into designated classroom activities to differentiate learning.

Teaching creative thinking skills is another strategy for process differentiation. The gifted education specialist teaches creative thinking and reasoning to students as it applies to specific academic areas, thus improving the transfer of learning. The classroom teacher takes advantage of these newly developed creative thinking skills to enhance classroom learning with differentiated activities, test items, and group discussions. For example, a chemistry teacher conducting a lesson on how two different elements combine to make a compound might ask more advanced students what would change after substituting one element for another.

Another method of process differentiation includes teaching research and investigative skills. Many gifted learners enjoy working more independently than other students at grade-level. Teaching process skills of a particular field of study (methodologies) gives gifted learners tools for independent studies as they develop highly specialized, real-world skills within a discipline. In a collaborative model the gifted education specialist can teach investigative and research methods to target students. Later, classroom teachers can rely on these skills to develop independent studies with individual or small groups of advanced learners. For example, while average ability students are studying journalism, the specialist could teach investigative writing to advanced learners. Gifted learners could then use these skills to conduct investigations of their own.

Product Differentiation

The outcome of learning that a student demonstrates as a result of processing specific content is called the product. When educators have made content and process modifications in the curricula, they should differentiate gifted learners' work products as well. There are a variety of ways to offer students differentiated work outcomes including rubrics, offering authentic product options, and allowing students to self-select products.

The practice of developing and implementing graduated rubrics facilitates differentiated learning in mixed-ability classrooms. Typically, a rubric consists of criteria for evaluation and a continuum of performance given each criterion. A graduated rubric provides various levels or ranges of outcomes given the criteria listed. The rubric reflects the level of learning and expected outcome. The benefit of a graduated rubric is that it allows for varying entry and exit points in any given learning experience and promotes continuous progress or learning for high-end learners. After planning the rubric collaboratively with the classroom teacher, the gifted education specialist should develop and implement the high-end learning rubric.

Authentic products directed at real audiences also serve to differentiate learning for advanced learners. Work products intended for real audiences require specific formats for production. A student who chooses to write an editorial versus investigative piece will learn different skills given the nature of the topic, intended purpose, and target audience. In a Resource Consultation and Collaboration Program, the classroom teacher can rely on the specialist to differentiate student work products by teaching related production skills for product completion and identifying real audiences to provide feedback on the students' work products. When targeted students are able to "buy out" of the regular education curriculum, the gifted education specialist can teach the production skills necessary for various work products as well as supervise students working on alternative work products within the classroom.

Perhaps the easiest form of product differentiation is to allow for various forms of expression as part of student production. Students can select their own products (either on their own or from a list generated by the classroom teacher and gifted education specialist) using their strengths, interests, and abilities as guides. This type of product also forces students to create their own sense of appropriate formats for specific outcomes. When students select a particular work product format, the intended audiences for student work shifts from the teacher to a wide range of possibilities. Although easy to conceive, monitoring many different products within any given classroom can be time-consuming and exhausting for the teacher who must teach production skills, monitor student progress, and evaluate end products. However, a collaborative approach allows the classroom teacher to share responsibility for developing, implementing, and assessing a variety of student work products with the gifted education specialist. The gifted education specialist can teach specific production skills and support and monitor advanced students' development of work products while the classroom teacher focuses on regular classroom students' products.

Differentiated Lessons

Typically, whole group learning is not effective in a mixed-ability classroom. Advanced learners often quickly finish their work, only to have to wait for the rest of the class to catch up before they can move on. To accommodate a mixed-ability group of learners, educators can adapt the introduction and culminating experiences to accommodate all types of learners, but they should differentiate intermediate lessons to meet the needs of students with different levels and rates of learning. When differentiating lessons for gifted learners, educators need to consider a four-step process described by Wooster (1978):

1. Whole group introduction of material.
2. Gifted learners participate in limited practice for mastery.
3. Gifted learners participate in extension of learning or advanced progression to next level of study.
4. Whole group culminating activity.

All students can begin a lesson with a basic introduction of new material, but because gifted students learn at an advanced pace, they will need less practice. Educators should then compact the core curriculum so that target students can pursue in-depth studies of advanced content. At the end of the unit, all students come back together in a culminating activity that builds on all levels of mastery and the various outcomes from the differentiated lessons. Because gifted students are still part of the regular classroom and work on activities related to the core curricula, they can demonstrate advanced understanding for all students in the classroom. The gifted education specialist should develop a differentiated graduated rubric for the culminating activity, allowing all students to perform at levels commensurate with their varying abilities.

Figure 5.1 presents an example of a lesson in its traditional form and after it has been differentiated to meet the needs of gifted learners.

Curriculum Differentiation Strategies

As educators begin to learn to differentiate lessons, they must keep in mind that differentiated experiences are distinct from the regular curriculum and not more of the same type of learning exercises in which average-ability students engage. Activities should challenge and engage gifted learners who have already mastered material, not just keep them occupied until the rest of the class is ready to move on. In a Resource Consultation and Collaboration Program, educators can use several strategies to provide differentiated educational experiences to students.

Demonstration Teaching

Gifted education specialists can occasionally deliver demonstration lessons for regular classroom teachers. Because it requires only a limited amount of work on the part of the classroom teacher, demonstration teaching is a good way to begin collaborating and build up a

General Education Lesson	Differentiated Lesson
Topic: Whales • *Voyage of the Mimi* • Literature • Workbooks • Video • Science explorations	Topic: Whales • *Man & Whales Investigation* • Problem-solving groups (overhunting, destruction of habitat, pollution) • Youth Summit (panel discussion, moderators)
Topic: American Revolution • Social studies textbook • Video • Children's theater (Constitution workshop)	Topic: American Revolution • Investigations (personal impact of the War of Independence) • Character study (historical character, literary character) • Novel (*My Brother Sam is Dead, 1776*) • Minuteman reenactment
Topic: Mythology • Genre study (mythology across cultures, fantasy) • Archetype study (heroes, trickster, antagonist, protagonist) • Greek Week Festival (performance)	Topic: Mythology • Investigations (ancient Greece) • Simulation (Greek city-states, government, gods and goddesses) • Greek Week Festival (performance, literary reactions)

Figure 5.1. Sample general and differentiated lessons.

comfort level with the processes. The lesson also allows the classroom teacher the opportunity to recognize and identify gifted behavior in students while he or she is observing (rather than delivering) the lesson. These lessons should be differentiated and must involve the classroom teacher at some point. For example, the gifted education specialist can plan a challenging lesson that is connected to the core curriculum. When delivering the lesson to the entire class, some students will reach an intellectual plateau before others. The classroom teacher and specialist then divide the students into groups for the end of the lesson in order to continue challenging students who need it and allow other students to practice mastery.

Tiered Lessons

Creating tiered lessons allows teachers to design instructional activities that address the diversity among student ability levels within the heterogeneous classroom. While developing and implementing multiple lessons within a classroom can be time consuming and difficult at times, in a collaborative and consultative approach, the gifted education specialist can help the classroom teacher plan, implement, and follow-up at least one tiered lesson, the lesson that addresses the needs of advanced learners.

Higher-Order Questioning

Raising the level of teacher and student questioning during regular education instruction can differentiate learning for gifted students. Varying the level of student questions is important in any whole group lesson, especially in the introduction and culminating activities. During lessons, the classroom teacher and gifted education specialist can deliver different levels of questions while co-teaching, or the gifted education specialist can differentiate the level of questioning for advanced learners in written activities or tests.

Small Groups of Intellectual Peers

The stimulation of same-ability peers during instructional activities is essential for healthy socio-emotional development in gifted learners. Flexibly grouping students during instruction along with providing differentiated learning experiences address the advanced cognitive and affective needs of gifted learners. Small groups of same-ability students provide levels of challenge that enhance the differentiated learning experience. Further,the success of some instructional strategies (e.g., Socratic Seminar) depends on the number of student participants.

Individualized Instruction

Although gifted learners have much in common with one another in how they learn, there is great diversity across this group of learners. Therefore, educators must consider individualized instruction when developing educational opportunities most appropriate for gifted learners. Some of these strategies include interest and learning centers, small group and team investigations, supplemental curricular resources and materials, and specific differentiation approaches.

Interest and Learning Centers: Interest and learning centers or stations in the classroom offer gifted learners access to challenging learning activities in the general education classroom and allow students to work at their own pace. Students progress through station activities after they complete other assignments or in place of assignments that are not appropriately challenging. The classroom teacher and specialist work together to plan tiered lessons and other activities for centers that address gifted students' advanced learning rate, but the gifted education specialist takes the lead in developing the activities. The specialist also monitors student progress by assessing student performance and providing meaningful feedback to students.

Individual or Team Investigations/Independent Study: Students of similar ability and interests work together to pursue in-depth and sophisticated studies and projects. The gifted education specialist assigns group membership and task responsibility based on individual students' needs and interests.

Contracts for Individualized Study: In student contracts, educators individualize learning by designating what the student will learn, the level of expected outcome, and a timeline for completion based on the core curriculum and student interests and learning needs. In a collaborative model , the gifted education specialist helps develop and monitor learning contracts as well as assesses student performance and intermittently provides feedback on continued progress.

Mentors: Advanced learners often have acquired knowledge and competency as well as interests that are above their current grade level. A mentor or professional in the field of the student's interest can help the student pursue complex and sophisticated learning through real-world, advanced, and complex content. Mentors can meet with students in their classrooms, at the mentor's job site, or over distance using e-mail and the Internet. The gifted education specialist supervises the relationship.

Dual Class Enrollment: Often a student's individual learning needs are so advanced that differentiating lessons is necessary almost daily. In this case, students should move to another classroom at a more advanced grade level on a part-time basis (e.g., for one subject area). For example, high school students may be enrolled in high school and college-level courses simultaneously. A Resource Consultation and Collaboration Program can make dual class enrollment work within an elementary school as well. When there are cluster classrooms across grade levels, a gifted learner that needs acceleration in a particular subject moves to another cluster classroom at a higher grade level where he or she can work with same-ability peers. For example, a fourth-grade student working at very advanced levels in language arts can attend enrichment lessons in language arts that the gifted education specialist teaches to high-ability fifth-grade students. The gifted education specialist plans and monitors the students involved in dual class enrollment.

Supplemental Materials and Resources

Most general education classroom materials are not entirely appropriate for gifted learners. The material's content, reading level, flexibility, and pace or rate of progression may not be appropriate for gifted learners at all. While compacting the curriculum might include using some of the regular classroom resources at an accelerated pace of learning, supplemental materials that replace or supplant classroom materials are critical to the success of differentiation. The gifted education specialist should provide supplemental materials and resources for classroom teachers based on the standard core curriculum to encourage transfer of learning. These materials and resources are not a tack-on to existing materials; instead they replace and extend core curriculum materials. A student who has demonstrated mastery should not have to complete math problems in the standard textbook before using supplemental problem-solving materials. While providing these replacement resources is an important part of a Resource Consultation and Collaboration Program, educators should keep in mind that the materials alone are not sufficient for providing appropriate differentiated opportunities for gifted learners; they are simply tools for doing so. Below is a list of resources that are particularly helpful in co-teaching situations:

- Replace grade-level materials with advanced texts and references. When advanced learners develop interests in advanced topics, problems arise with finding developmentally appropriate instructional materials, as grade-level materials lack the depth and breadth of information that gifted learners are capable of studying. Using technology, above-grade-level textbooks, and resource materials can support advanced levels of learning and interests in all academic areas.

- Use literature programs such Great Books® to supplement or replace grade-level language arts texts. These programs should use challenging instructional models such as interpretive questioning or literacy circles.

- Use novels to replace basal readers. Gifted learners can explore above grade-level reading material in place of grade-level materials through novel studies that are coordinated by the gifted education specialist and/or the classroom teacher. Additional strategies for reading advanced novels include studying novels in a series and replacing reading groups with book clubs. All collaboratively planned differentiated reading efforts can take place in the regular classroom or via complimentary lessons taught by gifted education specialist.

- Bring community, library, and other resource materials on loan to the classroom. Often advanced learners need access to resources that are written for older children or adults to explore and develop their areas of interest and sophisticated understanding. The gifted education specialist should collect and organize materials for advanced students around upcoming units of study in the general education classroom.

- Recruit appropriately challenging mentors and speakers for regular classroom lessons. Collaboratively, the gifted education specialist and classroom teacher can locate and invite professionals with in-depth knowledge about a unit of study into the classroom. Students with sophisticated interests can pursue in-depth learning with these mentors in school and/or through technology (e.g., e-mail, video-conferencing).

- Use problem-solving programs to supplement math curriculum. To enhance the complexity and abstractness of math studies advanced learners encounter, students can get involved in problem-solving programs when time is bought out of the regular math curriculum. Although the gifted education specialist may initially work directly with students building their competency in problem-solving, classroom teachers can differentiate activities for gifted students based on these problem-solving skills.

- Use hands-on construction materials (e.g., Lego®s) to enhance math and science programs for students who possess knowledge and competencies about math and science beyond their chronological age. The gifted education specialist can lead these programs when students have bought out of regular classroom activities.

- Rethink how to use available curricular or software programs such as Hands-on Equations®. Although these programs may not be geared specifically for gifted learners, they can allow for advanced study. For example, a student can use software programs that may be written for remediation if they allow the student to progress at his or her own pace through the various levels of the program. Students can work on these programs in the regular classroom or under the supervision of a media specialist, technology teacher, or the gifted education specialist (depending on where the computers are available).

- Develop lessons around real-life problem solving and problems-based learning to increase the sophistication and complexity of any topic. The gifted education specialist can develop real-life problem-solving challenges around the general education curriculum, and classroom teachers can implement the activities alone or collaboratively with the specialist.

- Use software to extend courses of study. Software programs such as SimCity™ and Internet resources such as Ask Jeeves™ extend learning for students who pursue independent studies. A growing number of distance education opportunities (e.g., online courses) are available and can extend learning for advanced learners who are able to work independently or in small groups. The gifted education specialist can develop and monitor activities around the core curriculum that take advantage of such technology resources.

- Supplement the curriculum with mini-courses, modules, and other similar learning materials. After compacting the curriculum to buy out time from general education activities, students can work individually or in small groups on mini-courses (e.g., online courses), simulated learning projects (e.g., Interact® Simulations), and educational contests.

- To supplement learning in any discipline, use biographies to study both high achievers in specific disciplines and the discipline itself. For example, studying experts in a field allows students to see the career choices and decisions the experts made to succeed in their field. Biographies can also provide students with a different perspective on historical events.

- Give gifted learners access to career resources at an early age. The gifted education specialist can assist classroom teachers in integrating career guidance information and activities into the general education classroom.

- Supplement the curriculum with "how-to books" that illustrate the methodologies of various disciplines of study. The gifted education specialist should provide teachers with resources that assist gifted learners in developing competency in the methodologies of disciplines that they are studying. The specialist can also teach methodologies in complementary lessons or incorporate them into independent studies that high-ability learners pursue in the regular classroom.

- Supplant portions of the general education curriculum with appropriately challenging competition programs. The gifted education specialist can establish competitive programs (e.g., Math Olympiad) and help classroom teachers compact the curriculum to make time for more challenging competition program activities.

Classroom Management Strategies for Supporting Differentiation

The nature and structure of the classroom determines the ultimate efficacy of any curricular or instructional intervention. Because differentiating curriculum and instruction is imperative to the education of gifted learners, schools must develop supportive learning environments that enhance rather than inhibit these modifications. For example, a group of twenty highly verbal students cannot engage in a meaningful Socratic discussion because the large number of students precludes in-depth discussion by all participants. Similarly, students will not develop individual interests when the topics of their studies are always predetermined by the teacher. The learning environment either enhances or inhibits the differentiation of curriculum and instruction. Therefore, it is vital that educators practice good instructional management that allows for an appropriate learning experiences.

Assessing Student Mastery Levels and Compacting the Curriculum

Curriculum compacting is the practice of diagnostic-prescriptive teaching. It begins by pre-assessing students' mastery levels through informal and formal assessment strategies. Teachers should determine student mastery level of curriculum content at the beginning of each new lesson or unit, and there are a variety of ways to determine mastery level. Teachers could use a student's proficiency test, practice test, or achievement test results to determine mastery level. Other assessment methods rely on performance-based activities such as having a student read aloud to establish his or her reading level. It is important to remember, however, that students need the opportunity to review the content to be tested before they take the actual test.

Pre-assessing students can seem like additional work for an individual teacher. In a Resource Consultation and Collaboration Program, assessing student mastery often works more smoothly than it might in other program settings. While the classroom teacher presents an introductory lesson, the gifted specialist can observe students for gifted behavior that indicates pre-existing knowledge or the capacity to learn new material at a more advanced level and/or faster pace. Conversely, the gifted education specialist might present a demonstration lesson while the classroom teacher observes student behavior. Further, the gifted education specialist might have access to pre-assessment instruments and strategies more appropriate for the assessment of readiness at the level of gifted learners. This collaboration takes the responsibility for determining mastery off of one teacher's shoulders and spreads it over two, making it much more appealing to classroom teacher.

Pretesting or pre-assessing a student's current status and cumulative knowledge base in specific areas of study helps teachers determine what students already know as well as how to differentiate curricula appropriately. With this knowledge, educators can base instruction on students' current levels of understanding of the content, and students then have to participate in learning only what they do not know, rather than what they already know. This technique helps gifted learners buy out time from the general education curriculum to participate in differentiated learning. Although the practice of compacting is not different in a collaborative approach, it is more efficient because more than one teacher is involved. Classroom teachers more readily use compacting when the gifted education specialist is available to assist in assessing student mastery and preparing, implementing, and evaluating differentiated learning experiences.

Increase Student Autonomy

Advanced learners have an inclination for independent learning that educators must develop and nurture. Student autonomy helps gifted learners realize their full potential by setting a path for lifelong learning. So many young gifted students' interests and aptitudes are above that of their same-age peers that learning commensurate with their advanced levels must be independent of other students their age. Therefore, autonomous learning becomes a necessity for students who spend a lifetime learning at levels beyond their chronological age.

Although there may be a natural inclination to learn more independently than other students their age, educators must strive to develop these skills in high ability students in ways that are appropriate. They must provide students with frameworks for autonomous learning and specific skills for production at a level commensurate with students' advanced abilities. Once students have developed these skills, a variety of instructional activities throughout K-12 education and beyond open up. Independent study, individualized programs of study, independent research, and self-directed learning become possible strategies for delivering differentiated learning experiences.

In a Resource Consultation and Collaboration Program, autonomous learning has several important implications. First and foremost, the gifted education specialist is responsible for developing and nurturing any inclination high-ability students have for autonomous learning. Second, classroom teachers must respect and address this inclination, and both the gifted education specialist and classroom teachers must work together to provide appropriate modifications in curriculum. Third, helping students develop skills in autonomous learning can facilitate specific service delivery strategies implemented in and out of the regular classroom such as independent studies and research.

Use Self-Management Strategies

Self-evaluation and management are important skills to cultivate for the socio-emotional development of gifted learners. Gifted learners are more intrinsically motivated than other students their age and can benefit from appropriate self-evaluation and monitoring techniques that keep this locus of control in check. Students who don't understand appropriate self-monitoring could develop fear of failure, perfectionism, or other vulnerabilities.

Developing skills in self-evaluation and monitoring is an important part of differentiated learning experiences. Being able to look to themselves for evaluation instead of relying solely on the teacher allows students to work more independently. Students can learn to set appropriate goals, organize materials, monitor their rate of progress, manage time, and appropriately evaluate work quality or products throughout the instructional activity.

In a Resource Consultation and Collaboration Program, self-management is particularly important. The gifted education specialist cannot supervise all differentiated experiences, nor are classroom teachers able to do so. Therefore, the specialist must develop, implement, and monitor strategies for having students check their own work, manage instructional activities, and share input in the assessment of their work. For example, the classroom teacher and gifted education specialist may develop differentiated activities for target students to work on in the regular classroom. Students can check their work by a visiting the specialist's folder (kept by the classroom teacher). The gifted education specialist monitors students' work folders and provides individual feedback. When a group of students experiences similar problems, the gifted education specialist can pull them together for brief periods of direct instruction.

Conclusion

The ultimate purpose of any gifted educational programming, regardless of the service format, is to provide appropriate differentiated educational experiences to gifted learners. Collaborative efforts focus on individualizing the curriculum and providing differentiated lessons and supplemental differentiated curricular materials for those lessons. A Resource Consultation and Collaboration Program allows gifted learners to engage in differentiated experiences more frequently than other service delivery formats because the gifted education specialist and classroom teachers can share responsibility for all students who show potential as well as the workload associated with those target students. Figure 5.2 lists additional resources to help school staff develop and implement differentiated curriculum and instruction for gifted learners

---

Educational Resources for Developing and Implementing Differentiated Curricula

- Renzulli, J.S., Leppein, J. H., Hays, T. S. (2000). *The multiple menu model: A practical guide for developing differentiated curriculum.* Mansfield Center, CT: Creative Learning Press, Inc.
- Renzulli, J. S. (1995). *Schools for talent development: A practical plan for total school improvement.* Mansfield Center, CT: Creative Learning Press, Inc.
- Tomlinson, C. A. (1999). *The differentiated classroom: Responding to the needs of all learners.* Alexandria, VA: ASCD.
- Tomlinson, C. A. (1995). *How to differentiate instruction in mixed ability classrooms.* Alexandria, VA: ASCD.
- Winebrenner, S. (1992). *Teaching gifted kids in the regular classroom.* Minneapolis, MN: Free Spirit Publishing.

Figure 5.2. Resources on differentiating the regular curriculum.

Exemplary Differentiated Lessons Delivered Through Resource Consultation & Collaboration

Consultation and collaboration is a service delivery strategy, and its effectiveness depends on the quality of the differentiated learning experiences that go along with it."—Project Consultant

Resource consultation and collaboration is a service delivery approach that is only as good as the differentiated learning opportunities it provides. This chapter contains sample small and whole-group differentiated lessons, learning contracts, and independent studies for gifted learners. The variety of formats presented here illustrate the various possibilities for delivering high-quality differentiated lessons in a Resource Consultation and Collaboration Program.

Planning Differentiated Lessons

During regular co-planning sessions, classroom teachers and the gifted education specialist (along with any other necessary support personnel) plan differentiated lessons. This planning occurs in short, regular sessions and occasional long-term planning sessions.

The Starting Point

Planning for curriculum differentiation starts with the regular education curriculum. The differentiated lesson should be an extension of the regular curriculum that concentrates on in-depth study and/or enriches the regular curriculum.

Building the Foundation

Before classroom teachers and the gifted education specialist can plan differentiated lessons and activities, they must first assess students' mastery of the regular classroom. Based upon pre-assessment scores, educators can collaboratively group students according to mastery level and compact the curriculum for the high-end learners. The gifted education specialist and the classroom teacher then plan differentiated learning experiences based on the core curricula for students to complete in the time that has been bought out by compacting the regular curriculum.

Choosing the Lesson Format

Teachers and specialists work together to determine the format for differentiated lessons. Time, resources, expertise, and student grouping will have impact on the type of lesson chosen. For example, the gifted education specialist could pull students from the regular classroom for differentiated instruction or provide a demonstration lesson to the entire class. Co-teaching would be another option. Of course, any one lesson could incorporate several different formats, especially given that the lesson may last several days.

Follow-up

The follow-up to the lesson is important. The teacher and gifted education specialist may choose to assess student knowledge or provide opportunities to continue study in the topic. To help students continue study, the gifted education specialist can provide the classroom teacher with a learning/interest center, develop student contracts, guide independent studies, or develop a combination of any of the three.

Collaborative Efforts for Compacting the Curricula

One of the goals in providing differentiated learning opportunities through collaborative efforts is to prevent add-on work to the regular curriculum. While it is a priority to integrate differentiated activities with the regular education curricula, it is essential that teachers allow students to buy out time from the regular curricula so that they are not responsible for work related to differentiated activities on top of regular curriculum work. Following are several scenarios for structuring class time to incorporate differentiated opportunities. All of the scenarios occurred in schools in the Charlotte-Mecklenburg School District in Charlotte, North Carolina.

Scenario One

At Elizabeth Lane Elementary School, the fourth grade classroom teachers responsible for the high-ability math sections compact the math curriculum into three days a week and co-teach with the gifted education specialist, Sallie Dotson, the remaining two days of each week. The classroom teachers work with Mrs. Dotson to design and administer pretests that will indicate which students can participate in the compacted or compressed curriculum. Typically, students must obtain 94% mastery to be released from the full course of study. The format for the co-teaching days varies and may include interdisciplinary math projects built around a grade-level theme, a math lab for a small group of students, or individualized instruction for a given child.

Scenario Two

In Sharon Elementary School, the gifted education specialist, Lea Harkins, and the classroom teachers work together to compact the curriculum. At the beginning of each new unit of study, the classroom teachers and Mrs. Harkins design and administer pretests to all students. Pretesting students before each unit maintains the fluidity of student groupings. Once students are targeted for alternative instructional lessons, the classroom teachers and Mrs. Harkins schedule instructional time across all of the classrooms within a grade level. For example, if math is taught at 10:30 a.m., the gifted education specialist will teach an advanced, differentiated math lesson for high-ability students during that time. As differentiated lessons are scheduled, Mrs. Harkins determines the method of delivery with classroom teachers. The lessons might consist of any or all of the following:

1. direct instruction in the resource room for students with gifted behaviors,
2. independent contracts for students to work on during designated times in the regular classroom,
3. learning centers placed in the regular classroom and/or in the gifted education specialists' resource classroom, and
4. acceleration and/or enrichment activities.

At other times, the differentiated educational opportunities might consist of more frequent sessions spent on more, in-depth parallel units of study that the specialist develops. For example, while the general education teacher focuses on geography in the Western Hemisphere, Mrs. Harkins will teach a simulation, Museum of the Americas, in which students create a living history museum that reflects the various cultures of people living in the Western Hemisphere.

Scenario Three

University Park School uses annual midyear curriculum-based assessments in math to place students in advanced-level math classes. Every student in a given grade level takes these tests in January and May. Because these tests are based on state curriculum standards, the results indicate which objectives in the standard course of study in mathematics the students have mastered. The gifted education specialist, Ms. Wheeler, plans differentiated learning opportunities to replace instruction in the classroom for objectives that students have mastered. Some of the lessons are cotaught in the regular classroom, and Ms. Wheeler delivers others in the resource room.

Scenario Four

Intraclassroom grouping across each grade level creates one top math group in one or more classrooms. The top math group teachers compress the regular curriculum into four days each week and turn to Mrs. Bissell to provide the differentiation in their classroom on the fifth day. Children in lower grades that perform at extremely high levels occasionally join the highest performing group at the next grade level for more challenging learning experiences. Some students are placed in higher-level classrooms on a regular basis, but the grouping remains flexible in that it accommodates students who enter or exit this group only for certain lessons based on assessments of mathematics aptitude.

Exemplary Small and Whole Group Differentiated Lessons

In a Resource Consultation and Collaboration Program, classroom teachers and the gifted education specialist develop differentiated lessons together with any other necessary staff members. The classroom teachers, the gifted education specialist, other staff members, or a combination of educators deliver lessons to students in small groups, whole groups, or by classroom. The following exemplary collaborative lessons illustrate how good differentiated curriculum and instruction for gifted learners can be delivered.

Lesson One: Photo Math Culminating Activity

This lesson developed out of weekly co-planning sessions between the two third-grade teachers with the highest math groups and the gifted education specialist. It served as a culminating activity to extended learning on geometry. It was conducted in class during the regularly scheduled mathematics class. The math teachers and the gifted education specialists are weaving the theme of patterns into all mathematics study for this year. Some earlier lessons in this particular math unit on geometry focused on the relationship of geometry to the concept of patterns. While planning is a joint effort between the classroom teachers and the gifted education specialist, the gifted education specialist takes the lead in creating the handouts (including the student performance rubric) that the students work through to complete the activity. To introduce the activity, the gifted education specialist presents an overview of the assignment to the entire class as well as a student performance rubric so that students know the expected criteria for their performance (see Figures 6.1 and 6.2). Then, the classroom teacher and the gifted education specialist each take half of the class (each high ability group one at a time) through the same lesson. The lesson takes several class meetings to complete. First, the groups take a walking tour of the school and campus to identify objects to measure and photograph. All students in both groups tour the school and outdoor surroundings with either the specialist or teacher acting as guides. Each student independently selects one object along the tour. Second, students move at their own pace through other activities outlined in the student handout. The classroom teacher and specialist work with students individually as each student completes the tasks. At the conclusion of their work, each group shares their results with one another. Either the classroom teacher or the gifted education specialist uses the rubric to assess student performance for students in their groups and provide a grade for this activity.

Lesson Two: Geometry Project

While the classroom teacher, gifted education specialist, and art teachers plan this differentiated successive teaching pull-out lesson, the gifted education specialist takes the lead in developing and implementing the lesson. The group of educators develop this lesson to provide enrichment opportunities for the group of students at the second highest ability level in math, and it follows the classroom teacher's introduction of geometric concepts to the class as a whole group (see Figure 6.3). Based on standardized testing scores, the classroom teacher

PhotoMath Culminating Activity

Task: Identify patterns and relationships that show the connections between geometry, measurement, and fractions. Create a photography display that clearly communicates your learning experience.

Project Components: Your display must include:
- A photograph of a unique object at school that can be measured safely, fully photographed, and is an identifiable geometric shape
- Display of data showing accurate dimensions of the object in real life and in the photograph
- Accurate use of metric and U. S. systems of measure
- Mathematical comparison of the object's dimensions in the photograph and in real life.

Shape Research

Directions: For your research, you will use only regular polygons. The regular polygons are listed below. You will need to list the number of sides for each polygon. You will then need to cut out, paste, and label an example of each polygon on a separate sheet. Organize your cut-and-paste sheet in the same order as the list below.

Name of Polygon	Number of Sides
Triangle	____
Rectangle	____
Rhombus	____
Trapezoid	____
Parallelogram	____
Pentagon	____
Hexagon	____
Heptagon	____
Octagon	____

Object Research

Objects to Photograph	Safety	Shape's Name	Photographic Capability
_____	____	_____	_____
_____	____	_____	_____
_____	____	_____	_____

Measurement Data

Dimensions of Real-life Object	length_____ width_____
Dimensions of Object in Photograph	length_____ width_____
Mathematical Comparison	length_____ width_____

Identify the relationships you see in the space below.

_____

_____

_____

Figure 6.1. Student instructions for PhotoMath culminating activity.

Rubric for PhotoMath Activity

Directions: Check the appropriate performance level for each criterion.

Criteria	Performance Level	
Photograph of unique object	____ met	____exceeded
Accurate display of data	____ met	____exceeded
Appropriate graphics	____ met	____exceeded
Accurate mathematics	____ met	____exceeded
Shows understanding of content	____ met	____exceeded
Creative solutions to task	____ met	____exceeded
Worked with constant focus	____ met	____exceeded

Comments:
Student _____

_____

Teacher _____

_____

Reflections:
Think about how you approached and handled this project and answer the following questions:
How did you decide what to photograph?
What did you try in order to find mathematical comparison?
What are some examples of relationships that you discovered?
What do you really understand about what you learned?
What are you still confused about?

Figure 6.2. Rubric for PhotoMath culminating activity.

determines which students need to have a more challenging learning experience, and, therefore, participate in this out-of-classroom experience with the gifted education specialist. Targeted students have their regular curricula compacted collaboratively by the classroom teacher and gifted education specialist to give them time to work on this project in a small group with the gifted education specialist and in class with the classroom teacher when time allows. This particular lesson allows gifted learners to build on the general education math and social studies curricula by studying advanced geometry and architectural building designs in the students' home town. During one specified math class session, the art teacher helps students learn ad-

---

Geometry Project

You have been hired to design and construct a building for an architectural firm. You will build a three-dimensional model for the building out of student-made materials. (For example, you could build a house out of sugar cubes, pretzel sticks, or cereal boxes but not Lego®s.) The firm would like you to include the following in your project:

- at least 4 plane figures
- several space figures
- several congruent figures

You should mount your model on a piece of poster board and neatly type or write your name on the front. Be ready to name the plane figures, space figures, congruent figures, and describe your building orally. Be creative and have fun!

Figure 6.3. Student instructions for geometry project.

vanced concepts such as perspective, planes, and solid figures. While the advanced students work on this lesson in math, their classmates work on similar topics and grade-level objectives. The specialist provides the grade on the project using a rubric that she created alone.

Lesson Three: *Recycling Gazette*

To plan for the differentiation of the core curricula (math, language arts, social studies, and science) for high ability students in fourth and fifth grades in a self-contained, multi-age classroom, the classroom teacher and gifted education specialist meet weekly. Because of the advanced ability levels of the students in this unique classroom, most of the curricula is either compacted or supplemented with more rigorous differentiated experiences. Often, the two educators select in-depth, multi-disciplinary projects to differentiate the core curricula. The gifted education specialist takes the lead in designing a research project for the class on recycling. The entire class works in small groups or individually on activities focused on investigating recycling issues more deeply than they would in the regular science curriculum. The specialist helps students identify questions about recycling and guides their independent research. Students mostly work during class time under the watch of the classroom teacher. At the conclusion of their studies, students break into groups to create original products that report what they find in their research efforts. The classroom teacher and gifted education specialist work with separate groups to help them develop a project according to a mutually agreed upon student product rubric. Under the guidance of the gifted education specialist, one particular group of students elects to develop a newsletter. The students write the copy and create a layout with help from the technology teacher who comes into the classroom to work with this group of students. The specialist makes arrangements for several mentors to work with students on the writing aspects of the newsletter. The group makes copies of the newsletter and distributes it to the entire student body of the school.

Lesson Four: Hawk Research

Third-grade students in a self-contained, high-level math class work through a multi-disciplinary approach to advanced studies, and this particular lesson builds on the regular curriculum in technology, social studies, and mathematics. Typically, the grade-level curriculum for this high-ability math class is compacted into three days a week, and the gifted education specialist and the classroom teacher work together in weekly planning sessions to provide differentiated instruction on the remaining days. The gifted education specialist meets separately with the technology teacher to consult on this project development as well. After the class completes a compacted unit of study on measurement, the students then have seven consecutive days of math class in which they complete this in-depth research project.

At the time this lesson is implemented, third-grade students are studying indigenous animals and prey to the North Carolina region in which the students live. At the same time, students are working on developing research and problem-solving skills with the gifted education specialist. To bring the two areas of study together, the classroom teacher, gifted education specialist, and technology teacher develop a project that asks students to research the wingspan of a hawk (school mascot and indigenous bird of prey). The gifted education specialist takes the lead in developing guidelines for student work and creating a student product rubric. The math class is divided into small groups of students that work together to complete the project. The classroom teacher and gifted education specialist both facilitate group work. Once students gather measurement data on the hawk, the specialist rotates groups into the technology lab to work with the technology teacher on using computer software to graph data. After graphing their data, students create a visual representation of their work using technology to plot the data and create a poster to present the data and implications of the data for display. Each group presents its final project to the class and places it on exhibit. The gifted education specialist and the classroom teacher use a product rubric to rate each final project and provide a mathematics grade for each student. (Figure 6.4 presents the student instructions and evaluation rubric.)

Hawk Research Project

Task: Use thorough research about our school mascot, the hawk, to plan and create a school-wide mathematics display. Be sure to name different kinds of hawks and describe the hawks in our hometown.

- Required Components:
- Accurate research
- Accurate measurement
- Accurate estimation
- Visuals with appropriate graphics
- Student involvement
- Clear communication

Evaluation Rubric

Criteria   Rating

- Accurate research   _____
- Accurate measurement   _____
- Accurate estimation   _____
- Visuals with appropriate graphics   _____
- Student involvement   _____
- Clear communication   _____

Activities:
1. What did you already know about hawks?
2. What questions do you need to ask?
3. Describe the following about your hawk:
   - physical characteristics   • food
   - habitat   • predators
   - other
4. Write your personal reflections about the following:
   - Something I learned that I can use outside of schools
   - Something I learned about my thinking
   - Some examples of relationships that I discovered

Figure 6.4. Student instructions and rubric for Hawk Research project.

Lesson Five: Mountain Valor

Fourth-grade students are grouped by ability for language arts, and all of the high-ability students are served in one classroom. The gifted education specialist works with the highest-ability students to further differentiate the literacy experience. Based on standardized test scores in reading and writing, the specialist and classroom teacher decide which students will work on a differentiated novel, and this differentiated work supplants the traditional reading program for the grade level. The specialist makes the literary selections and plans and implements the lessons, sharing her work with the classroom teacher during weekly co-planning sessions. The specialist delivers the differentiated lessons in the classroom during literacy class time or in pull-out sessions conducted during literacy class time. This particular fourth grade language arts pull-out lesson is conducted through collaborative teaching with the gifted education and general education teachers to initiate the lesson. After the introductory lesson, students complete independent work in the regular classroom during language arts instructional time (see Figure 6.5). The specialist makes periodic impromptu visits to the classroom during language arts to check on student progress. Students keep all of their work in folders so that the specialist and classroom teacher can check on their progress and provide feedback to students. The specialist provides language arts grades for students based on their small group work conducted during the cotaught lesson and independent work completed on their own.

Mountain Valor

This section of *Mountain Valor* takes readers from 1862-1864. Due to the Civil War, many changes have taken place on the McAimee farm. Valor is growing up with only Savannah to guide her, since Valor's mother never recovered from the fall that you read about in Chapter One. Valor still believes that she is a sister to the wind, and she still longs to prove that she is as courageous as her father.

Activities:

Chapter 6 — This chapter continues the episode of the Blaylock visit and describes the birth of a foal. Summarize the events of this chapter.

Chapter 7 — This chapter holds the story of the book jacket illustration. Read the chapter carefully and write a paragraph explaining whether or not you think the illustrator read the book before drawing the cover illustration.

Chapters 8-12 — These chapters take place in 1864, and they emphasize the plight of a runaway slave and her two children. Summarize these chapters and decide whether or not Jed and Valor acted ethically.

Valor really hates having to act like a lady! In these chapters, she disguises herself as a boy. Make a chart contrasting how she must dress/act as a lady and the way she dresses/acts as a boy.

Vocabulary — Find three unfamiliar words in each chapter and define them. Choose two of the three to use in a sentence.

Challenge — Find the location of the following Civil War battlefields: Gettysburg, Spotsylvania, Cold Harbor, Fort Donelson, Shenandoah.

Figure 6.5. Student instructions for *Mountain Valor*.

Lesson Six: Paul's Ride Paraphrased

This small group project is a differentiated lesson for gifted fifth-graders to complete in the regular classroom in place of designated language arts activities. It is an example of using a contract to guide small group projects in the regular classroom rather than the resource room under the guidance of the gifted education specialist. During bimonthly planning sessions, the gifted education specialist and the classroom teachers determine which aspects of each language arts unit will need differentiation for high-ability learners. Although the gifted education specialist and classroom teachers (each who has a cluster of high ability students in her classroom) all discussed this lesson, the specialist develops, implements, and evaluates it. While the classroom teachers guide the regular class through several pieces of literature, including "Paul Revere's Ride" by Longfellow, the students with the highest standardized test scores in language arts, especially in reading comprehension, participate in the differentiated activity. The gifted education specialist introduces the project in her resource room (see Figure 6.6), but students conduct most of the work in the regular classroom with 20-minute follow-up visits to the resource room twice weekly so that the specialist can monitor students' progress through the activities listed on the contract. The students keep their work on the contract in folders that the gifted education specialist checks daily. The gifted education specialist develops and implements a rubric (provided to students in a handout) to evaluate and grade student work.

Paul's Ride Paraphrased

Paraphrase a specific section of "Paul Revere's Ride" by Longfellow. After thorough planning, produce a group product that communicates the original text and your paraphrase.

Criteria:
- Clear, accurate communication
- Computer generated
- Appropriate graphics
- Use of expert computer skills
- Displayable product
- Produced as a group

Figure 6.6. Student instructions for Paul's Ride Paraphrased project.

Lesson Seven: Historical Novel about North Carolina

The fourth-grade students in this school are heterogeneously grouped across all classrooms for social studies and science, with clusters of eight to ten identified gifted learners in several classrooms. The fourth-grade teachers meet daily to plan lessons, and the gifted education specialist joins these sessions once a week to plan for differentiation in social studies and science. In one session, the gifted education specialist and the classroom teachers with gifted students look at a social studies unit and decide to develop a multidisciplinary project focused on writing and social studies. They determine which introductory, whole group lessons are critical for student learning and which lessons will be replaced with the on-going independent project (for targeted students). The teachers and gifted education specialist plan the project together, but the specialist draws up guidelines for the project as well as the student product rubric. The independent project guides students through writing an original novel that accurately portrays historical events and includes a creative dimension unique to each student's work (see Figure 6.7). Highly-able students work in a small group with the gifted education specialist in the resource room two or three times a week as well as during class in place of specific social studies assignments. The classroom teacher makes sure that students follow the guidelines for the project but does not provide instruction. The gifted education specialist uses a specified rubric to evaluate the final product and provide a grade to the classroom teacher.

Lesson Eight: Science Fair Projects

In this particular school, students are grouped by ability for math and language arts, but homeroom teachers teach science and social studies to heterogeneously grouped classrooms. Most classes contain ten to fifteen identified gifted learners and other high ability students. The gifted education specialist meets with the classroom teachers once a week during their grade-level meetings to plan for differentiated science and social studies lessons.

This particular independent study involves a third-grade science research project. The science teachers want students with exceptional ability to develop sophisticated research skills in science. To introduce the students to scientific experimentation, the teachers agree that they will create a mini science fair. The gifted education specialist develops and implements the lesson and evaluates student work. Third-grade students devise and work on laboratory experi-

---

Historical Novel

Task:
- Create an original novel.

Components:
- Choose an historical setting in our state.
- Choose an historical event in our state.
- Determine the main character.
- Decide on the story line (beginning, middle, end; problem, solution).
- Use illustrations.

Activities:
- Write the novel.
- Publish the novel.
- Share the novel.

Student Deadlines:
- List below your deadlines for the each task in the project.

Rubric for Evaluation:
My evaluation level is _____ because _____

_____

Evaluation Levels
4=Wow!!, 3=I Met the Challenge, 2=I Can Do Better, 1=I Must Do Better

---

Figure 6.7. Student instructions for Historical Novel project.

ments independently in class during curriculum buy-out time and in pull-out sessions with the gifted education specialist in the resource room. When the students finish their projects, they share their findings with one another. The gifted education specialist provides student assessment based on a predetermined rubric.

Lesson Nine: Fiction Book Club

Because language arts is taught to heterogeneous groups of students, classroom teachers with clusters of eight to twelve identified gifted children meet weekly with the gifted education specialist to plan and implement differentiated learning experiences for high-ability learners. Cluster teachers asked the gifted education specialist to help them by providing them with more challenging literary experiences for highly-able readers. The gifted education specialist designs book clubs for grades three through five. Most of the reading selections are at least one grade level above the current grade level status for any given child. Classroom teachers from the same grade level send their highest readers to the resource room where the gifted education specialist meets with students once or twice a week. Students also work on assignments related to the book club in the regular classroom when time permits, and the specialist creates a set of guidelines for independent student work in the classroom (see Figure 6.8). The classroom teachers keep students on task, but they do not provide instruction to students regarding reading selections. The gifted education specialist periodically visits classrooms to monitor student progress. The specialist receives and reviews all finished assignments and provides grades for the targeted students.

Fiction Book Club

Student _____

Novel _____

Genre _____

Vocabulary Product _____

Comprehension Product _____

Complete the following questionnaire about the current book club novel on a separate sheet of paper.

1. Give a description of the main character, including name, physical, and/or personality characteristics.

2. Write, in detail, about the setting of the story, including the name and place.

3. What is the main problem in the novel and what is its solution?

Figure 6.8. Student instructions for the fiction book club.

Exemplary Differentiated Learning Contracts

Often classroom teachers consult with the gifted education specialist to develop learning contracts for advanced learners. These contracts replace classroom lessons deemed inappropriate for gifted learners, and teachers and students readily use contracts for several reasons. First, when gifted education specialists are not present in a given school building on a daily basis, contracts allow educators to provide differentiation to gifted learners regularly. Second, teachers like the quick access to differentiation that contracts provide. Third, the gifted education specialist likes the in-depth learning that takes place when students accumulate time (by buying out of regular class work) to work on contract assignments.

Contract One: Myths and Legends

In this school, the gifted education specialist co-plans with classroom teachers every other week to differentiate the regular curriculum in core areas for high-end learners. This learning contract complements the regular education, fifth-grade language arts unit on myths and legends. While most of the differentiated work in language arts is done in the resource room, educators decide that this particular unit requires only moderate changes to the core learning experiences. The classroom teachers and gifted education specialist agree that a learning contract will provide target students with differentiated experiences whenever time allows in the regular unit of study. The gifted education specialist develops the contract after discussing it with the classroom teachers. The contract (see Figure 6.9) contains a number of activities, and the number of activities a student might complete is related to the degree to which the student needs to extend core curricular activities. The gifted education specialist initially presents the contract to students in the resource room and continues to meet with students once a week to check their progress and provide instruction as necessary. The weekly small group sessions also give participating students time to interact with one another while working on the contract. The specialist also periodically checks on the students while they are in the regular classroom. Students keep designated work folders so that the specialist can take the materials with her, provide written feedback, and return the work to the students between work sessions in the resource room. The specialist develops an assessment rubric and evaluates the final work project. The project grade is included in the classroom language art's grade for that grading period. This cooperative teaching activity is an example of complementary teaching, whereby the gifted education specialist develops and implements a unit individually that complements the unit that the classroom teacher is presenting to non-gifted learners.

Contract Two: Go Fly A Kite

The gifted education specialist and classroom teachers identify several fifth-grade math students with accelerated math abilities. Their on-going mathematics study is a combination of whole group class lessons, pull-out enrichment with the gifted education specialist, and individualized skills development using computer software. Standardized testing and

Myths and Legends Contract

Vocabulary:

- Define each of the words. Your definitions should focus on a myth or legend.

Myth	Antagonist
Legend	Villain
Hero/Heroine	Theme
Protagonist	*add _____ words

- Compare and contrast the characteristics of a myth and a legend using a Venn diagram.

Reading:

- Read ___ books all together. ____ should be about myths, while ___ others should be about legends.

Activities:

1. After reading your myths and legends, choose ___ to explore a little more deeply.

2. Choose at least _____ activities from the following list to complete and deepen your understanding of the literature.
   - Give a book talk to the class.
   - Poetically retell the myth or legend.
   - Create your own myth or legend.
   - Choose a character that visits you. Write an essay entitled "I'll never forget the day I met _____."
   - Create a timeline that sequences the events of the story either in pictures or writing.
   - Create an artifact from the myth or legend and explain its importance.
   - Create a story map using graphic organizers.
   - Create a time capsule from the setting of your myth or legend. What would be included? Why? Include at least 4 items, and explain each in an essay.
   - Create a comic strip to retell the story.
   - Write an authentic puppet show to retell the story.
   - Research a popular game/activity from the culture. Teach it or perform it for the class.
   - Come up with an activity idea of your own.

Evaluation Rubric:

Criteria	Rating
On time	_____
Oral Presentation	_____
Knowledge	_____
Neatness	_____
Creativity	_____
Thoroughness	_____

Ratings
1=below standard; not acceptable   2=adequate effort; some missing pieces
3=meets the requirements; complete; neat   4=superior; above expectations

Figure 6.9. Myths and legends student contract.

curriculum-based assessment via interactive computer software provide specific assessment information on the current status and needs of these fifth-graders. The purpose of this contact is to provide an enrichment experience that extends and broadens the mathematics program.

The current math curriculum unit focuses on geometry, and the gifted education specialist develops a contract that encourages students to develop a viable kite using elements of geometric design and creative thinking (see Figure 6.10). Students work on this project with the gifted education specialist in the resource room during regularly scheduled math time as well as in the regular classroom. (When the small group meets in the gifted education resource room, an extremely precocious first-grader joins the fifth-grade students to complete some aspects of the contract.) They also work with the gifted education specialist to create a self-evaluation of the contract rather than using a predetermined rubric. The gifted education specialist evaluates the students' work and provides a math grade on the final work to the classroom teacher.

> **Go Fly A Kite Contract**
>
> **Objective:** The student will design and make a kite to share with classmates and other students. The student will demonstrate geometry skills and creativity through elaboration.
>
> **Resources:**
> - NCTM materials
> - Classroom and public library materials
> - Classroom art materials
>
> **Time frame:** 10 days
>
> **Requirements:**
> - Accurate graph paper rendering of kite design
> - Use of math knowledge and skills (scale, measurement, geometry, etc.)
> - 3-D model
> - Actual flying ability/potential
> - Originality

Figure 6.10. Go Fly a Kite student contract.

Contract Three: Accelerated Performance

Several third-grade classroom teachers ask the gifted education specialist to develop a differentiated math experience that would be available in the classroom for students who demonstrate the need for more challenge in math at any given time during the current unit of study. This contract leads individual children through a menu of possible extension activities and consists of both required activities as well as optional activities. Students can complete all of the activities in the regular classroom in place of designated regular education activities, but students may need to make a trip to the resource room to pick up some materials necessary to complete them. To check on student progress, the specialist makes periodic visits to the classroom during a time frame the classroom teacher chooses. The specialist evaluates student performance using a rubric and provides a math grade to the classroom teacher.

Contract Four: Countdown to End of Grade Tests

This contract (see Figure 6.11) differentiates regular education classroom instruction focused on preparing students for proficiency testing in second through fifth grades. Classroom teachers spend as much as two weeks annually preparing for the end-of--year proficiency tests,

---

Countdown to End-of-Grade Tests Contract

10. Locate 3 specific skills (based on your proficiency test results) to practice.
9. Complete 5 sessions (30-45 minutes) on the Josten's Learning Path (computer program).
8. Proficiency test activity.
7. Participate in an in-class activity.
6. Work one-on-one with the gifted education specialist.
5. Proficiency test activity.
4. Proficiency test activity.
3. Work one-on-one with a parent volunteer.
2. Play two math games.
1. Practice exponents and numeration.

Figure 6.11. Countdown to End-of-Grade Tests student

and gifted students work on this contract while the classroom teacher works with the rest of the class on test preparation. The gifted education specialist and classroom teacher examine existing standardized test scores and curriculum-based assessment to determine who should participate in contract activities. The contract is designed so that any given student will work on proficiency test preparation only in the areas warranted. The gifted education specialist designs a contract that any classroom teacher in grades two through five can use to differentiate any academic area being tested. The gifted education specialist introduces the contract to advanced students and monitors progress, but students complete most of the activities in the regular classroom. Students do not receive grades on this contract.

Contract Five: Energy Task

During weekly co-planning sessions, fifth-grade teachers and the gifted education specialist decide that some parts of an upcoming energy unit need to be differentiated for high-level learners who have a strong familiarity with the topic. The gifted education specialist designs and introduces a contract (see Figure 6.12) that provides alternative learning experiences during the unit. To determine who will participate in the contract, the gifted education specialist teaches a higher-level lesson

---

Energy Task Contract

Choose one of the following forms of energy as a focus for the activities: nuclear, mechanical, chemical, thermal, radiant, and electrical.

Activities:
Collect evidence to prove the following big ideas about your form of energy.
- Energy can change forms.
- The total amount of energy does not change.
- The sun is the source of all energy.

Develop your evidence into a visual presentation that may include charts, diagrams, experiments, and your ideas.

Figure 6.12. Energy Task student contract.

to the entire class so that the classroom teacher can take note of students with advanced ability in this area. Targeted students participate with the whole class during the introduction of the unit to renew their familiarity with the content. Afterword, they work on the contract in place of other whole group activities. The classroom teacher and gifted education specialist design a rubric to assess the final visual presentation that students develop and provide science grades for contract participants.

Lesson Six: Olympic Games Statistics

Part of the on-going differentiation of fifth-grade math experiences provides students with advanced applications of skills presented in the core mathematics program. During regular co-planning sessions, the classroom teachers and gifted education specialist decide that an upcoming unit on graphing would not challenge the most capable mathematics students in the high-ability classroom. The gifted education specialist suggests a contract that would differentiate most of the learning experiences presented in the regular curriculum instructional unit (see Figure 6.13). The gifted education specialist works with a small group of identified students in the resource room two to three times a week, and students also work on contract activities in the regular classroom. The multidisciplinary contract combines advanced research skills, graphing skills, technology, and social studies and requires students to create a series of graphs based on primary and secondary sources that reflect some aspect of the Olympics from 1896 through 1998. Given the nature of the contract activities, students can work on the contract during social studies in addition to math if deemed appropriate. Students can seek help from the classroom teacher, gifted education specialist, media specialist, and the technology specialist. The gifted education specialist develops a rubric to assess student portfolios of graphs and provides mathematics grades to the classroom teacher.

Olympic Games Statistics Contract

Task: Using primary and secondary resources, collect statistical data about the Olympics over time. Develop a portfolio of graphs that communicates your learning.

Criteria for Evaluation:
- Use of a variety of primary and secondary sources
- 6 complete graphs in portfolio (3 hand-made and three computer-generated, including pie, bar, and line graphs)
- Statistics that reflect the idea over time (as early as 1896-1998)
- Professional display format for portfolio
- Use of appropriate and unique graphics
- Excellent time-management

Figure 6.13. Olympic Games student contract.

Exemplary Differentiated Independent Investigations

Independent studies are another example of indirect services the gifted education specialist can provide. They are individualized projects that students can complete at any designated time with general education teachers and/or gifted education specialists guiding student work rather than a student contract. The most unique aspect of these independent investigations is the time students spend interacting with other advanced peers. The following independent studies outline various collaborative approaches to these investigative studies. Each is conducted with a small groups of students.

Independent Study One: Biography

Fourth-grade classroom teachers and the gifted education specialist plan weekly to develop and implement differentiated literature experiences for students with above-grade-level aptitude (as determined by standardized test scores) in reading. The differentiated experiences are a combination of in-class and pull-out activities, and this independent study provides in-class activities that replace the regular education literature program with differentiated experiences (see Figure 6.14). The general education teacher and gifted education specialist collaboratively plan the independent study, but the gifted education specialist implements the investigative process. The independent study involves self-selected readings, guided journal entries, and culminating activities all focused on biography. During regularly scheduled language arts class, students work in small groups and independently in the regular classroom and meet with the gifted education specialist for assistance once or twice weekly. The gifted education specialist provides a language arts grade for this work.

Biography Independent Study

First read your selected text. While you are reading, you will need to note any vocabulary words that you do not understand. Also, place in the attached sheets the facts that you come across about your person.

Instructions:
1. Divide a sheet of construction paper into four parts. You will then talk about each major event that happened in that person's life.
   - Section One: Gather information about the early years and record three or four phrases that apply to that person.
   - Section Two: Gather memorable experiences that occurred during the second major period of his or her own life.
   - Section Three: Record any major developments, struggles, or achievements.
   - Section Four: Record any information concerning the final years. Remember to include some of the reasons why this person will always be remembered.
2. Set up a personality trait rating for your character. Brainstorm all behavior that your character exhibits. Then decide if they are positive or negative behaviors. Give the behaviors a rating of 1-5 and explain why you have assigned the ratings.

Journal Topics:
- Is this someone you would like to have grown up with? Why or why not?
- Pretend that you are this person's brother or sister. Explain how you feel about him or her.
- What do you think was this person's greatest accomplishments.
- Pretend you bump into this person on the sidewalk. How would you act? What would you say?
- Which teacher in school do you think would be most proud of this person? Explain why.
- A newspaper has decided that the person you read or wrote about is its person of the week. What would the newspaper say about this person? Write this information in a short essay.
- Create a dialogue between you and your person. Make sure that you have meaningful questions to ask.
- Answer the following questions:
  - Who do you know or know of that reminds you of this person? How are they alike? How are they different?
  - Why should other people read this book?
  - What was the most difficult thing this person ever had to do?
- Select stories about this person that were funniest, saddest, happiest, and most unbelievable.
- Think of a situation that happened to a person in the biography and write about how you would have handled the situation differently.
- Using the information from the book, write five headlines that could be used in a history book.
- Describe the impact or role this person and/or event has had on society.
- Consider how this story can help you in your own life. Explain.
- Do you think a biography should have been written about his person? Explain your answer. You need to cite specific sections in the book by page number to support your position.
- What do you remember most about this person's story? Why?
- How did you feel while reading this book? Why?

Activities:
- Design a place mat about your book.
- Write a poem based on the book.
- Design a book jacket for the book.
- Create a timeline of 10 major events in the person's life.

Figure 6.14. Independent study on biography.

Independent Study Two: My Community Tic-Tac-Toe

This independent study for second-grade gifted learners in the regular classroom supplements the regular education social studies curriculum. Both the gifted education specialist and classroom teacher feel that some of the students in the class are capable of a more complex exploration of an upcoming social studies unit focused on North Carolina history, and together they develop an independent study to meet these students' needs. Students identified as gifted and other students from the talent pool participate in the independent study. The students first participate in whole group introductions to North Carolina history in the local region. In place of other whole group instructional activities, participating students select three activities outlined in the independent study matrix that the gifted education specialist has created (see Figure 6.15). The classroom teacher makes sure that students progress through the independent study and allows students to work together or individually. Periodic small-group meetings in the resource room with the gifted education specialist helps students complete projects. The gifted education specialist and classroom teacher collaboratively

My Community Tic-Tac-Toe		
Directions: Choose any three activities across, down, or diagonally.		
Survey twenty people and ask them what would make our hometown better for young people. Graph the results.	Illustrate a postal stamp that would commemorate our hometown.	Choose a landmark in our hometown and write a story about its importance to the community.
Locate an important business in our hometown. With an adult's help, find out more about it. Take notes.	Write a letter to the mayor or civic leadership organization asking for information.	Use pictures to show our hometown's recreational or cultural opportunities.
Collect pictures and ads from the newspaper that showcase people from our hometown.	Design a model of one of our town's skyscrapers.	Find out where much of the new commercial and residential growth will emerge. Show your findings on a map.

Figure 6.15. Community Tic-Tac-Toe independent study matrix.

review students' final work and provide a social studies grade for the independent study.

Lesson Three: Aztec Civilization

In planning for differentiated learning experiences for high-ability learners in fifth grade, the classroom teacher and gifted education specialist decide to provide a long-term independent study during the nine-week grading period. Both educators feel that most of the upcoming units in social studies can be compacted for target students. The gifted education specialist and classroom teacher pre-assess the entire class and compact the curriculum accordingly. Based on ability levels, students receive some whole group social studies activities, usually those that introduce new concepts, but in place of other regular classroom activities, they complete the independent study that the specialist has planned (see Figure 6.16). The independent study activities require students to prepare a research paper, visual display, and presentation. Students work independently in the regular classroom with a time line that outlines student goals by weeks, periodically going to the resource room with the gifted education specialist for assis-

---

Aztec Civilization Independent Study

<u>Directions</u>: State your paper's topic, theme, generalizations, and areas of focus. Explain that this paper will attempt to find evidence to support the generalization.

<u>Activities</u>:

Culture	Identify characteristics of the Aztecs and their values. Characteristics include religion, music, arts, food, and cultural celebrations.
Government	Looking through the eyes of an historian, sequence important conflicts in the Aztec's government over time and create a timeline.
	• Briefly explain the past government.
	• Briefly explain the present form of government.
	• Describe the parts of the government system.
	• Create a timeline of events in government.
Environment	Judge how the Aztecs used natural resources, looking at this question from both an environmentalist's and an historian's point of view.
	• Include an elevation map and other topographical maps.
	• Identify the Aztecs' natural resources.
	• Explain how the people used their natural resources to make a living.
Economy	Note the economic patterns of the Aztecs' over time.
	• Type of economy
	• Imports and exports
	• Currency
Summary	Explain what you have proved/disproved in this paper. With your visual, show how systems interact in the Aztec culture, government, environment, and economy. Be specific and support your argument with facts, examples, and details.

<u>Final Project</u>:
The final project will include a visual display, a research paper including a title page and bibliography (with at least 6 resources), and an oral presentation. You will be the school scholar, and your work will be kept in school as a "Museum Exhibit."

<u>Evaluation Criteria</u>:
- Title page
- Bibliography of 6 or more resources
- A 3-dimensional visual including all 4 parts of this research paper. These items will be included in a museum exhibit in the Learning Gallery.

<u>Timeline</u>: 2-3 months
Week one: gather resources and make contacts
Weeks two-four: begin research and interviews; take notes
Week five: begin rough draft and editing

Week six: develop a bibliography
Week seven: complete final draft
Week eight: develop visuals
Week nine: practice final presentation

<u>Figure 6.16.</u> Guidelines for Aztec Civilization independent study.

tance. The classroom teacher and gifted education specialist evaluate student work weekly and provide social studies grades based on the criteria they established.

Lesson Four: Myths Independent Study

The gifted education specialist and fifth-grade classroom teachers plan weekly for differentiation in all core academic areas. This particular differentiated unit supplements a regular education social studies unit. Both classroom teachers and the gifted education specialist share in planning the independent study, but the gifted education specialist develops the guidelines, meets with students regularly to oversee their work, and assigns a final grade for completed work. The gifted education specialist first teaches a high-level, whole group lesson to the mixed-ability classroom on ancient civilizations. Based on responsiveness to this lesson, the classroom teacher and gifted education specialist identify students who demonstrate an interest, aptitude, and desire to participate in the independent study and who are capable of working independently. Students work through the list of required activities in the independent study and select myths to use with five related but separate activities (see Figure 6.17). The classroom teacher and gifted education specialist work together to assess student performance and assign social studies grades.

Myths Independent Study

Activities:

1. Collect myths from around the world, beginning with the ancient cultures such as Egypt, Greece, and Rome. Compile a collection and include the myths, visuals, and the culture of origin.
2. Trace these myths over time, and create a time line including their cultural origin. Analyze the influence of the ancient Greek and Roman myths on today's literature.
3. Plot the location of the myths on a world map, and label with a symbolic visual.
4. Choose a natural phenomenon and create your own myth including a unique visual.
5. In a clarification paper prove the generalization by using your research on myths. Include very specific facts to support your big idea.

Figure 6.17. Activities for Myths independent study.

Lesson Five: Computer and Communication Technology

The gifted education specialist and fourth- and fifth-grade classroom teachers recognize that some of their students need a greater challenge in mathematics. Therefore, the gifted education specialist develops and implements an independent study that combines mathematics and technology (see Figure 6.18). Students in fourth and fifth grades who show a high interest in technology and are able to buy out time from the regular curriculum to work on the activities. Although students in the regular classroom participate as well as gifted students, the gifted education specialist brings all participating students to the resource room to assist students and monitor progress. The entire project takes nine weeks to complete.

Computer and Communication Technology Independent Study

Activities:
1. Research computer technology over time, including famous people and inventions that may have changed the course of computer history and/or made valuable contributions to mankind. Create a timeline that includes visuals, dates, and facts. Continue the time line into the future using the past as a basis for your predictions.
2. Research careers in computer technology by interviewing in person, on the telephone, or on the Internet several computer scientists or technical experts. Create a brochure advertising these career opportunities and the requirements involved.
3. Create a web site that connects our school to other schools and generates interest in computer technology. Consult with the school technologist and do a practical service project for our school based on his/her recommendations.
4. Repeat these same steps for communications technology, or incorporate them when able.
5. As always, you must prove the generalization we are currently investigating, and you, of course, may want to prove more than one generalization using clarification writing with numerous facts, examples, and details.

Project Components:
- Visual display
- Research paper including a title page, bibliography (with at least six resources), and an oral presentation

Time line:
This independent study will last two to three months because of the scope of the topic. It will be altered as necessary and will be checked weekly by the gifted education specialist and the classroom teacher.

Week 1: gather resources and make contacts
Weeks 2-4: begin research and interviews; take notes
Week 5: begin rough draft and editing
Week 6: write a bibliography
Week 7: complete final draft
Week 8: develop visuals
Week 9: practice and present final oral presentation

Figure 6.18. Guidelines for Computer and Communication Technology independent study.

Lesson Six: Researching the Importance of Mathematics

This independent study combines higher-level research skills with the regular education mathematics content in the fourth grade. Classroom teachers design and conduct weekly informal pre-assessments of student skills so that they can then compact the math curriculum for high-ability math students. Following co-planning with classroom teachers, the gifted education specialist takes the lead in developing the guidelines for implementing an independent study that combines career education in mathematics, research, and the development of histograms (see Figure 6.19). Participating students complete the independent study during regularly scheduled math classes and regularly reflect on their work in a project journal. The gifted education specialist designs a student performance assessment rubric that is included in the independent study guidelines. The classroom teacher and gifted education specialist use the rubric to assess student progress and collaboratively assign a final mathematics grade for the independent study.

Researching the Importance of Mathematics Independent Study

Task: Gather evidence to determine the importance of multiplication and division in the lives of adults. Create a detailed histogram to display the results of your research. Draw conclusions from your histogram and look for evidence to prove the big idea.

Activities:
1. My Survey. Interview at least 10 adults regarding the two most important ways in which they use multiplication and division in their occupations. Record their responses.

Name	Occupation	Multiplication	Division

2. Histogram Conclusions.
   My histogram about _____ shows many facts. Some of the most important facts are:

   Since the facts I have listed are true, I can figure out some other things that are true by drawing conclusions. Some of my conclusions are:

Evaluation Criteria:

	Met	Exceeded
Completed survey	___	___
Plan for histogram	___	___
Completed detailed histogram	___	___
Excellent time management	___	___
Draws conclusions	___	___
Shows understanding of theme/generalization	___	___
Thoughtful reflections	___	___

Evaluation Levels
4=Wow! exceeds expectations   3=Met challenge well; met expectations
2=Can do better; partially met expectations   1=Must do better; met few or no expectations

Reflections:
While thinking about your own thinking, answer each of the following questions about your project in your journal.

1. Where did you get the idea for your title?
2. How did you decide to do graphics?
3. What other ideas did you try out while completing your contract?
4. What relationships did you discover?

Figure 6.19. Guidelines for mathematics independent study.

Conclusion

Perhaps the most difficult task in implementing a Resource Consultation and Collaboration Program is to develop meaningful differentiated learning activities. It is certainly one of the most time-consuming and training-intensive aspects of the program. The lessons described here represent exemplary collaborative and consultative efforts that model the processes at their best and serve to guide teachers in the process of curriculum differentiation. Educators can use these lessons as templates as they work to develop their own collaborative lessons.

Chapter 7

PROTOTYPE SCHOOLS WITH RESOURCE CONSULTATION & COLLABORATION PROGRAMS IN GIFTED EDUCATION

"Now we can do more for gifted kids, and that's how it should be."
—*Elementary School Principal*

Resource Consultation and Collaboration Programs in gifted education are adaptable to the strengths and existing structure of any school, and each program will be unique to the contexts of the school and its staff. The model schools described here are composites of efforts within programs from Charlotte-Mecklenburg School District in Charlotte, North Carolina and Charlottesville City Schools in Charlottesville, Virginia and illustrate the nature of programs given different applications.

The Charlotte-Mecklenburg School District is the largest public school system in North Carolina, with both an urban and suburban student population. Eighty-six elementary schools have developed Resource Consultation and Collaboration Programs. The student population is ethnically diverse, with a large minority student population. The collaborative approach follows a long-standing pull-out program that served students for a minimum of 90 minutes each week. In contrast, Charlottesville City Schools in central Virginia is a small school district with six elementary schools and one intermediate school using the Resource Consultation and Collaboration Model. The schools serve a bimodal population of students from high and low socioeconomic backgrounds and a large population of minority students. The district's previous service delivery model consisted of a center-based enrichment program that served students one day per week.

Elementary School Programs

Case One

Elizabeth Lane Elementary School in the Charlotte-Mecklenburg School District engages in the collaborative approach to serving gifted learners. Overall, the school population is very affluent and only moderately culturally and racially diverse. This particular school has a formally identified population of approximately 300 gifted learners in grades three through five out of a K-5 school population of about 1,000 students. The Resource Consultation and Collaboration Program serves approximately twice the number of identified gifted children. A full-time gifted education specialist, Sallie Dotson, works regularly with at least two teachers at each grade level (and two levels of high-end learners) as well as other staff. The building administrator, Anita Pangle, strongly supports collaboration and sets the direction for collaborative activities. When a recent review of student test scores revealed that a focus on mathematics differentiation was warranted, Mrs. Pangle created a schedule that allowed for weekly co-planning sessions between the gifted education specialist and teachers with the highest ability math and language arts groups in their classrooms. (All students are homogeneously grouped by ability for math and language arts instruction.)

Sallie Dotson has regularly scheduled weekly planning blocks with grade-level teams in grades two through five and works regularly with the high-ability classroom teachers for curriculum and instruction differentiation. She has a set schedule for participating in the instruction of the highest-ability math classes (of identified and non-identified students) in third through fifth grades and, when time is available, kindergarten through second grades. Every week, the classroom teachers with the two highest levels of math students compact their curriculum in order for Mrs. Dotson to provide at least two differentiated lessons. Mrs. Dotson and classroom teachers also practice co-teaching and team teaching on a regular basis. She regularly develops differentiated student product rubrics and assigns grades to student work completed while under her charge. Mrs. Dotson also leads a problem-solving program for high ability math students in grades K-5. Most often, she differentiates the language arts curriculum by using literary discussion techniques and alternative novels at students' advanced reading levels.

Mrs. Dotson often collaborates with several colleagues to develop interdisciplinary units. For example, when the third-grade teachers were working on measurement in mathematics and local animals in science, Mrs. Dotson taught students research methods and the technology teacher introduced graphing software. The teachers collaborated to develop a project in which the students researched information about hawks (measuring beak size, length, wingspan, etc.) in small groups, used computer software to graph their data, created posters with their research, and later gave presentations to the class.

The gifted education specialist works with individuals and small groups of students in all subject areas when classroom teachers have compacted the regular education curricula. Several individual or small groups of students come to the resource room to work on in-depth investigations in science and social studies.

Case Two

Providence Road Elementary School in Charlotte, North Carolina, serves approximately 350 gifted learners in grades two through five and over 1,000 students overall. The school has a bimodal population of students from low and high socioeconomic backgrounds. One full-time and one part-time gifted education specialist work with one teacher per grade level who then serves as a liaison to other grade-level teachers. The specialists largely serve students grouped by ability level in math and language arts and collaborate and consult with designated teachers.

The gifted education specialists, Leslie Spearman and Becky Workman, have regularly scheduled planning blocks with all grade-level teams. Teachers engage in cooperative teaching frequently, and on a daily basis, Mrs. Spearman and Mrs. Workman co-teach with those teachers who are assigned high-ability students in grades three through five grade for math and language arts. The high ability math and language arts classes are intraclassroom groupings of high-ability students. Within each group there are small clusters of extremely capable students. The specialists work with these students in small groups or with the entire high ability group on advanced content to infuse problem-solving into the program. In language arts, Mrs. Spearman and Mrs. Workman have students study novels as well as engage in other types of activities.

Collaboration activities often involve specialized school personnel such as the technology teacher. Mrs. Spearman provides direct instruction to small pull-out groups of second-grade students because they are typically spread across many classrooms when they are formally identified. She provides whole-class demonstration lessons in kindergarten and first-grade classrooms, and students in kindergarten and first grade also meet with her in small groups for enrichment lessons.

Once a week, the gifted education specialists also work with individual and small groups of gifted learners in specialized areas for enrichment. The students come from every classroom on a given grade level, and activities vary from book clubs to competitions such as Destination Imagination or Quiz Bowl.

Case Three

Sharon Elementary School in the Charlotte-Mecklenburg School District serves approximately 200-225 identified gifted learners in grades two through five within an overall student population of about 700 children. There are approximately ten to fifteen identified gifted students clustered in every classroom in second through fifth grades. The school has a bimodal population of students from low and high socioeconomic backgrounds. The school has a multiple intelligences focus and employs a full-time gifted education specialist, Mrs. Lea Harkins, assigned to kindergarten through fifth grade. An additional teacher, Mrs. Lucinda Dyer, works in a flow room (a concept related to the multiple intelligences focus of the school). Mrs. Harkins describes her collaborative work as "pull-out and push-in," referring to the environments in which teaching takes place. The specialists work together with classroom teachers to serve gifted students, students with disabilities, students with English as a second language, and all other students with specialized needs. The building administrator, Dr. Mary Martin, strongly supports collaborative services as a way to meet the needs of all students in her building. Dr. Martin not only makes accommodations, such as scheduling changes and implementing regular planning sessions, to support collaboration, but she also tries to win over reluctant or hesitant teachers. The school maintains professional development activities that support collaboration and differentiation strategies.

Mrs. Harkins has regularly scheduled planning blocks every other week with all grade-level teams in kindergarten through fifth grade. To conduct long-term, thematic planning for differentiation, she meets on a quarterly basis with grade-level teachers who have clusters of high-end learners in their classrooms.

The staff engages in a variety of co-teaching models. Classroom teachers with high-ability students clustered in their classrooms team teach with Mrs. Harkins. Other teachers engage in compliementary teaching, with the specialist pulling out students who have had the curricula compacted in order to participate in differentiated units. The classroom teachers then work with reduced classroom sizes. At the end of the lesson, the entire class of identified and non-identified students comes back together to work on a culminating activity supervised collaboratively by the gifted education specialist and the classroom teacher. Although differentiation occurs regularly in math and language arts, educators often use multidisciplinary units as well. For example, one differentiated mythology unit incorporated literature, music, and science studies.

Mrs. Harkins also works individually with students in kindergarten and first and second grade in both the resource room and in the classroom. The gifted education specialist delivers whole class demonstration lessons in the regular classroom and then pulls target students together from several classes to provide complementary lessons in the resource classroom. Small groups of students reading advanced novels, writing newsletters, or working on independent studies also come to the resource room routinely. Mrs. Harkins manages most of their work through contracts. Students can work on self-paced computer programs in the resource room and classroom.

Mrs. Harkins and Mrs. Dyer also support extracurricular programs for highly-able students. They both coach "Odyssey of the Mind" teams and provide other enrichment activities for any student demonstrating needs. School competitions as well as flow room activities are open to all students able to participate. During school-wide activities, at least two each year, Mrs. Dyer and Mrs. Harkins work as part of the instructional team, supporting opportunities for the creatively and academically talented.

Case Four

Eastover School in the Charlotte-Mecklenburg School District serves approximately 50 formally identified gifted learners in grades three through five and approximately 550 students overall. Most of the students served by the collaborative program are not formally identified as gifted students. The school is made up of children largely from low- to moderate-income families, and there is a great deal of cultural and racial diversity. The gifted education specialist, Barbara Bissell, works in this building two and a half days a week. While the building administrator, Mrs. Myrna Meehan, supports collaboration throughout the school, she clusters identified gifted learners across all classrooms at a given grade level, presenting a challenge to a specialist working in the building on a part-time basis.

In order to provide services to students spread across so many classrooms, Mrs. Bissell works with one teacher per grade level, who in turn serves as a liaison to other grade-level teachers. Classroom teachers also move students around classrooms to bring high ability students together, and the gifted education specialist sometimes pulls out target students for differentiated activities.

Collaborative planning sessions occur weekly with one cluster teacher per grade level, and educators develop a schedule of collaborative activity monthly. Collaboration involves all core discipline areas, with a focus on math and language arts, and differentiated learning activities are based on the required performance standards for each core academic area. On a regular basis, Ms. Bissell works closely with the school's literacy teacher to differentiate language arts lessons. Students read supplemental reading material at an advanced level, and Mrs. Bissell monitors the programs. She also uses a problem-solving program with high-ability math students in grades three through five.

Case Five

University Park School, a visual and performing arts magnet school in Charlotte, North Carolina, serves a population of 20 identified gifted learners in grades three through five. The student population is culturally and racially diverse, and the socioeconomic status of students varies greatly. Although many students demonstrate high performance on grade-level proficiency tests, most of the students served by collaborative efforts are not formally identified as gifted. The gifted education specialist, Sara Wheeler, serves this building only three days a week and works with approximately ten teachers. The building administrators, Mrs. Rosalyn Lackey and Mrs. Linda Kaiser, support collaboration and have worked hard to provide the specialist with additional time in the building so that she can increase the frequency of differentiated activities. Classroom teachers have weekly grade-level planning sessions, and Ms. Wheeler joins each grade level at least once a week. The greatest challenge in this building is that targeted students are spread across every classroom in grades two through five.

Although Mrs. Wheeler works with only one classroom per grade level in third through fifth grade, all teachers across grade levels plan together and with the specialist and share resources and instructional plans. The gifted education specialist spends her mornings co-teaching in cluster classrooms and afternoons collaborating with other teachers who compact the curricula. The classroom teachers pretest students at the beginning of most units and work diligently along with the specialist to provide on-going student assessment and placement in differentiated activities that are fully integrated with the core curricula. Most of the differentiated lessons take place with Ms. Wheeler in the resource room.

In addition to delivering differentiated instruction directly to targeted students, Mrs. Wheeler also provides classroom teachers with alternative materials and resources and regularly models differentiation practices during demonstration teaching. When the school collaborates on thematic, interdisciplinary units that incorporate the performing arts and academics, Ms. Wheeler also works with the staff to differentiate instruction for target students and include high-end learning activities as a part of these units.

By February of their second year of collaboration, the staff at University Park had provided as many differentiated activities as they had by May using a traditional pull-out service delivery model.

Case Six

McKee Road Elementary School in the Charlotte-Mecklenburg School District serves approximately 1,000 students in kindergarten through fifth grade. The school population is not racially or socioeconomically diverse. Most students are from affluent families and are of average to above-average ability. There two gifted education specialists in this building, Steve Houser and Jill Reicher, serve more than 400 formally identified students in grades two through five in mathematics, language arts, and science and provide differentiated lessons, activities and product rubrics. Mr. Houser and Mrs. Reicher each work with designated grade levels and approximately ten to twelve teachers each. An additional part-time enrichment teacher works regularly with K-1 students using a pull-out approach. Mr. Bill Pangle, the building administrator, is an ardent supporter of collaboration. In fact, the third enrichment specialist in the building is financially supported by the school, rather than by the district. Mr. Pangle supports sending classroom teachers to gifted education workshops that focus on differentiation and brings in consultants to provide professional development to the entire staff on related issues and topics.

At the beginning of each year, the specialists conduct whole classroom demonstration lessons. Soon after, teachers engage in cooperative teaching. Collaboration in this building also includes specialized school personnel such as the media specialist and art teacher.

The school groups most grade-level students by achievement levels for math, science, and language arts. Mr. House and Mrs. Reicher work with intraclassroom groupings of more than 25 high-ability students. Student placement in groups is mainly based on standardized tests, but the groupings remain fluid and, based on classroom performance, students can move into and out of groupings throughout the school year. Classroom teachers also pretest students to buy them out of regular classroom activities, and the specialist plans alternative assignments.

Mr. Houser or Mrs. Reicher join all grade-level meetings once a week for collaborative planning, using student performance standards as the basis for planning differentiated activities and lessons. The specialists and classroom teachers are developing specialized curricula in math and language arts for students in the top 5% of the class. The staff has also begun to create a scope and sequence of differentiated lessons across grade levels so that students can build on previous learning.

Case Seven

Lebannon Road Elementary School in Charlotte serves approximately 125 identified students in grades two through five. Students are racially and socioeconomically diverse. The gifted education specialist, Jill Reicher, works in the building full-time. The school clusters identified students in one classroom on each grade level in third through fifth grade. There are two special multi-age classrooms of highly-able kids in grades two through three and four through five. All but a few students in these classrooms are formally identified as gifted. Mrs. Pearlie Borders, the building administrator, is a vocal advocate for collaboration within the district, and she directed the development of multi-age classrooms for high-end learners.

Mrs. Reicher works with teachers who have clusters of gifted children in heterogeneous classrooms, as well as teachers with whole classes of high-ability math students. In order to group high-ability students together, teachers also move students from cluster classroom to cluster classroom for acceleration. Weekly co-planning sessions occur at grade level meetings, and collaborative efforts between Mrs. Reicher and the classroom teacher typically begin by conducting a whole group demonstration lesson. Mrs. Reicher also co-teaches to reduce the teacher-student ratio.

Mrs. Reicher leads students' independent studies as pull-out sessions in the resource room after teachers pretest students and buy out time from the regular curricula. Mrs. Reicher also spends a large amount of time in indirect service delivery by seeking out and providing supplemental materials to teachers. She is often seen rolling a cart of instructional materials to teachers during planning sessions or delivering resources to students in order to individualize their instruction.

Middle School Programs

Case Eight

Walker School in Charlottesville, Virginia houses a racially and socioeconomically mixed population of 700 middle school students in grades five and six. Teachers in the school work on dyad teams of two teachers from heterogeneous classrooms with small clusters of identified gifted students. One teacher is responsible for humanities and the other for science. At the sixth grade level, Mrs. Boyd is responsible for collaboration in the humanities, and Mrs. Tyrell is responsible for science. Similarly at the fifth-grade level, Mrs. Butts works with humanities and Mrs. Ely with science. The school groups students by achievement in language arts and math, and a math specialist conducts the high-ability classes at both grade levels.

The classroom teachers meet with the gifted education specialists by grade level and discipline on a weekly basis. The teachers and the specialists map out topics and design pacing guides for their disciplines for the entire year. They then develop concept-based units of instruction for the regular classroom. The gifted education specialist differentiates activities based on the concept-based curricula. The teachers also design pre-assessments for each unit to determine which students will work on differentiated activities in a given unit.

Differentiated lessons start with whole-group demonstration lessons followed by small group activities that take place within the regular classroom and in subsequent pull-out sessions. The gifted education specialists are responsible for developing student product rubrics and assigning grades for all differentiated activities.

Case Nine

A middle school in Northeastern Ohio serves approximately 1400 students in three grade levels. Approximately one-third of the student population is formally identified as gifted. The school groups identified students across teams within disciplines in 6 classrooms (two classrooms for each of the three grade levels).

The gifted education specialist largely provides indirect services to the cluster classroom teachers. She helps develop differentiated activities, collect and disseminate supplemental instructional materials to teachers, and creates differentiated student product rubrics. The main focus of differentiation is to extend the core curricula.

The gifted education specialist also hosts lunchtime enrichment activities for students, such as book clubs and debates. She provides short units on socio-emotional issues, career planning, and other topics for which students are dismissed from classes to participate. She also meets with individual students in one-to-one sessions and monitors individualized educational programs for specific students who require acceleration and other specialized services.

Case Ten

Crestdale Middle School from the Charlotte-Mecklenburg School District serves 1200 students in grades six through eight. The gifted education specialist, Phyllis Shaddock, works in the building full time. The school district is developing specialized curricula for advanced courses in each discipline area. For example, the district currently provides language arts teachers in sixth through eighth grades with an entire differentiated curriculum called "The Humanities of Language." Mrs. Shaddock works with teachers who have high-ability students to develop high-end differentiated instructional activities and provide on-going inservice training to teachers on topics related to curriculum differentiation. Mrs. Shaddock also joins team planning every other week to develop and work into the curriculum differentiated educational opportunities.

Prototype Classrooms

Classroom environments have a strong impact on the flexibility and success or failure of collaboration efforts. If educators do not take care in arranging classrooms so that individual or small groups of students can work effectively on projects while the classroom teacher works with the rest of the class, the gifted education specialist will be limited in the types of differentiated activities he or she can offer students. Likewise, if the gifted education specialist has his or her own room, he or she can easily pull students out of the classroom when necessary without worrying about whether space is available or not. Without a separate room, teaching arrangements are limited. This collection of vignettes illustrates supportive collaborative instructional environments.

Classroom One

During daily scheduled math instruction in Ms. Barbara Bissell's fifth-grade classroom, 30 high-ability math students (only eight students are formally identified as gifted) participate in a collaborative lesson. Approximately ten capable fourth-grade students from other classrooms join the class once a week because of their math aptitude. (Collaboratively, the teachers compact the regular math program into four days each week.) The lesson depicted here is part of an on-going problem-solving program that the gifted education specialist, Mrs. Sallie Dotson, and Mrs. Bissell co-teach once a week. The program promotes the introduction and mastery of specific problem-solving strategies so that students can integrate these skills into differentiated learning experiences across all disciplines.

Ms. Bissell and Mrs. Dotson meet once a week outside of the grade-level planning for about thirty minutes to plan the week's problem-solving lesson. Ms. Bissell and Mrs. Dotson determine how to compact the weekly lessons from the regular curriculum and divide responsibilities for doing so. They then plan the differentiated lesson based on the compacted curriculum and divide responsibilities for teaching. Finally, they develop a rubric for measuring student success in the differentiated problem-solving lesson.

The lesson begins with Mrs. Dotson introducing several new problem-solving strategies to the students as a whole group. Mrs. Dotson prepares a set of problems for self-paced folders that progressively become more difficult. Individually, students work through the folders using one of the new strategies. Students can use a variety of strategies to solve each problem, but they must determine which strategy best suits a given problem. While students move through the assigned problems at their own pace, Mrs. Dotson and Mrs. Bissell move around the class to work with individual or small groups of students who need help. As students finish each problem, they check the answer with Mrs. Bissell before proceeding to the next problem. Students are not expected to complete all the problems in one day.

In between weekly problem-solving lessons, students work independently, as time allows, through any remaining problems contained in the folder. Students continue to verify the accuracy of their responses with Mrs. Bissell, who has the answer key in a folder on her desk. Mrs. Dotson checks the classroom several times a week to assess student work and provide written feedback in student folders. In addition to the folders, Mrs. Dotson has developed a learning center that contains related activities on problem solving. When students buy out of regular classroom activities, they can work on their folders and/or spend time at the learning center. Because Mrs. Dotson is not always available, the center and folders allow for differentiation during math whenever it is needed. Figure 7.1 presents a diagram of the classroom's layout.

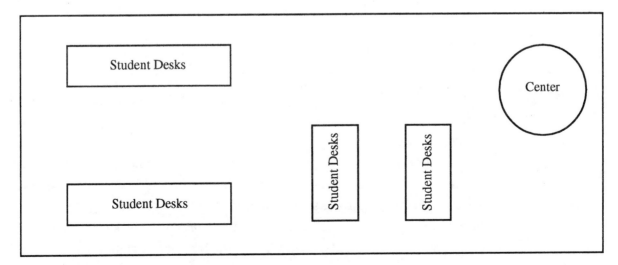

Figure 7.1. Diagram of prototype classroom one.

Classroom Two

Each Monday, Mrs. Murray, a fourth-grade math teacher, pretests students on the weekly topic of study. Based on the results, Mrs. Murray and Mrs. Payne, the gifted education specialist, work together to plan, implement, and evaluate student progress in differentiated learning activities.

At the beginning of the year, Mrs. Murray and Mrs. Payne map out the instructional units and topics for the year. They meet weekly for 45-60 minutes to plan for current math differentiation. Their mutual goals include planning for pre-assessment, developing differentiated learning activities around key concepts and skills, and creating differentiated student assessment rubrics to accompany various instructional activities.

For this lesson, Mrs. Murray prepares and delivers a twenty-minute introductory and overview lesson on a new math concept. Following the mini-lesson, Mrs. Murray gives an eight-item pretest to each student. She evaluates the tests as individual students complete them. Meanwhile, Mrs. Payne has developed and placed around the room station enrichment activities for students to work on after they have completed Mrs. Murray's pretest, and she guides student work at the centers as necessary. At the conclusion of the lesson, Mrs. Payne decides which students, based on their pretest scores, will complete the regular classroom or differentiated activities. Both Mrs. Payne and Mrs. Murray evaluate student progress and assign grades on core and differentiated lessons. The following diagram (Figure 7.2) represents the classroom during the weekly pre-assessment lesson.

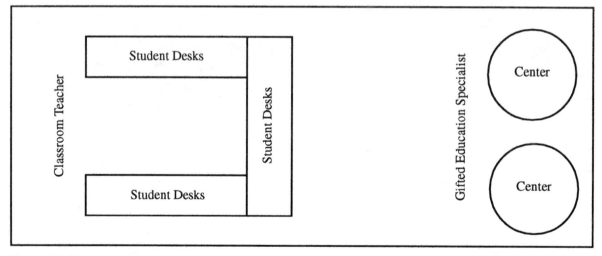

Figure 7.2. Diagram of prototype classroom two.

Classroom Three

This collaborative fifth-grade classroom is an inclusive environment in which students of greatly varying ability levels and needs are heterogeneously grouped together for all areas of instruction. Ms. Tienen, the classroom teacher, works weekly with the gifted education specialist, Mrs. Scharr, to plan, implement, and assess student progress in differentiated learning experiences.

Ms. Tienen decides which students have mastered the concepts and skills being taught and are ready for a greater challenge. Ms. Tienen works with Mrs. Scharr at the planning stage to develop ideas, but Ms. Tienen works alone to decide which students need differentiated learning experiences. Mrs. Scharr is responsible for developing and implementing the differentiated learning activities.

Because the degree of readiness for the unit test varies greatly among the students in this mixed-ability classroom, Ms. Tienen consults with the gifted education specialist for assistance in differentiating the review lesson for the unit test. While Ms. Tienen works with some students in the front of the classroom reviewing for a unit math test, Mrs. Scharr takes a small group of eight to ten top-ability students to the back of the room for an extension or enrichment activity on tessellations. After the differentiated lesson, Mrs. Scharr brings six to eight more students at the next highest math level to the back of the room to do a slightly modified version of the tessellations activity. There is no grading involved in the differentiated or classroom activities for the day. One student has an individualized math contract and works at the computer because his achievement level is below grade level, and he will not be taking the same test. Figure 7.3 presents the classroom layout.

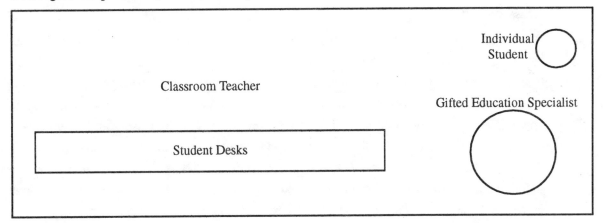

Figure 7.3. Diagram of prototype classroom three.

Classroom Four

In this particular classroom, Mrs. Harkins, the gifted education specialist, works with students who come to the resource room to engage in differentiated activities. Although she typically leads most lessons in the resource room, everything taught in the resource room is collaboratively planned with the classroom teacher and reflects the regular curriculum. The resource room can contain several different groups of students and/or individual students working on different projects simultaneously. For example, she may have fifteen to twenty first-grade students from several classrooms working in a small group while a separate small group of students from a fourth-grade classroom work on a spreadsheet project at six computers along the back wall of the classroom.

The first-grade classroom teachers are working on a math concept that many, but not all, students have mastered. While the classroom teachers teach the concept to students who have yet to master it, Mrs. Harkins provides an extension lesson to challenge the first-graders who have mastered the current math content. The first-grade teachers and Mrs. Harkins planned the date and time of the lesson collaboratively, but Mrs. Harkins developed the differentiated lesson alone. Mrs. Harkins will evaluate student success during the lesson activities and provide daily mathematics grades to the classroom teachers. Figure 7.4 displays the classroom setup.

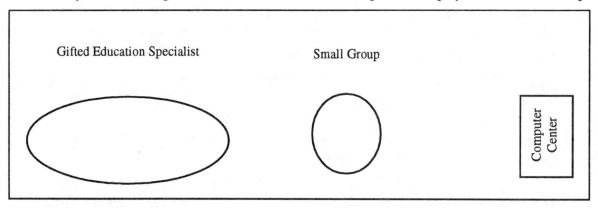

Figure 7.4. Diagram of prototype classroom four.

Classroom Five

In this school, one fifth-grade classroom teacher is responsible for high-ability mathematics instruction, and the gifted education specialist, Mrs. Lea Harkins, works with this teacher to provide individualized mathematics programs for targeted fifth-grade students and several younger students who work above grade level. Because of the students' advanced mathematical abilities, they spend at least three days on alternative work using an individualized mathematics program. Ironically, the specific mathematics program they are working with is typically used to develop deficient skills in low-performing students. However, because of the individualized nature of the program, it can also allow students to work beyond their current grade-level placement. The program provides an individualized assessment of student progress through skills development.

During math instruction, target students sit at the back of the room where they work individually on computers to complete the self-paced math program (see Figure 7.5). One fourth-grade student leaves his classroom to join the fifth graders at the computers at least once a week. The gifted education specialist periodically checks in with the students to monitor their

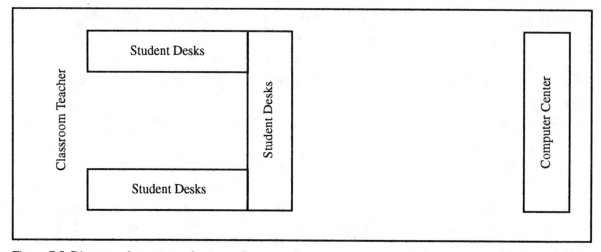

Figure 7.5. Diagram of prototype classroom five.

work and teach them new material. One day a week, a very young student works with the older students, and the older students serve as mentors to him. Mrs. Harkins provides grades for math studies for each student based on continuous progress through the computerized assessments of skill development.

Classroom Six

Mrs. Butts, the gifted education specialist, and the classroom teacher have co-planned a lesson on political cartooning. Although both teachers discussed the lesson, Mrs. Butts took the lead in preparing the student materials for the lesson. Mrs. Butts introduces the lesson to the class while the classroom teacher interjects and moves around the class facilitating student discussion. After the introduction, the two educators divide the class into two groups. Both teachers work with students on several exercises focused on understanding and creating political cartoons. While the classroom teacher leads most students in a group discussion, Mrs. Butts leads the advanced group of students in a higher-level discussion, almost a Socratic seminar, focusing on the concept of symbolism in cartooning. Both student groups work through group and individual activities, but the high-ability group works on activities that were modified to include symbolism. Mrs. Butts designed student rubrics for each group activity packet, and both teachers assign student grades for the members of their group. Figure 7.6 presents the classroom arrangement.

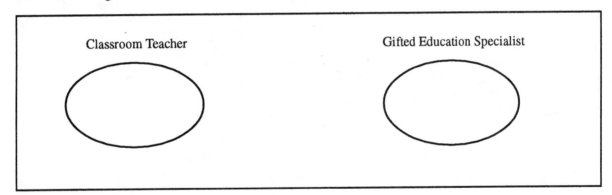

Figure 7.4. Diagram of prototype classroom six.

Conclusion

Just as schools implementing a Resource Consultation and Collaboration Program must make deliberate decisions about student grouping practices so that the gifted education specialists and classroom teachers can provide a wide range of differentiated activities, so too must they carefully construct classroom arrangements so that several teaching activities can take place at once. The scenarios described in this chapter illustrate that there is no one-size-fits-all arrangement. Each school must take into account its strengths and limitations and mold the program—student arrangements, teaching arrangements, and classroom arrangements—to make the most of the time, expertise, and facilities available.

PROGRAM POINTERS AND POTENTIAL PITFALLS

"It takes time to get the hang of all this, but it is really worth it."
—Classroom Teacher

Using resource consultation and collaboration practices in gifted education overcomes many of the problems with providing appropriate educational opportunities to gifted learners. It offers educators opportunities to address the needs of all high-ability students in their areas of competency, not just formally identified gifted learners. By encouraging educators to work together and by emphasizing a joint responsibility for high-ability students, the Resource Consultation and Collaboration Program takes advantage of the gifts and talents of an entire school staff, not just one or two people. And by building on the regular curriculum, the gifted education specialist and classroom teacher can work together to improve the transfer of learning and continuity of students' education.

However, educators should not enter into a program thinking that it will automatically raise the level of students' abilities or easily meet their needs. Developing a program requires commitment and determination and should be guided by careful deliberation and concern that the program start off on the right foot. In conclusion to this manual, several program pointers and potential pitfalls are outlined below. These ideas should serve as an easy reference to the basic requirements of a program and potential problem areas that are best addressed at the outset.

Program Pointers

Every Resource Consultation and Collaboration Program is different. One of the program's strengths is its malleability—allowing schools to conform the processes to and make the most of individual school situations. However, it won't mold itself. School staff need to make careful and deliberate decisions when establishing and implementing the program. The following nine strategies have proven to be universally successful in schools developing programs:

1. Schools must maintain flexible scheduling practices with teachers and students. The more flexibly students are moved around classrooms, the easier it is to offer

appropriately differentiated opportunities. However, to encourage more teachers to engage in co-planning, schools must establish schedules that build in regularly scheduled planning periods that fit with the gifted education specialist's demands on time.

2. Schools that use differentiated programs that span across grade levels facilitate resource consultation and collaboration practices. When teachers plan for differentiation separately for each grade level, they collectively spend more time at the planning phase of collaboration and less time engaging in co-teaching practices. The gifted education specialist must look for ways to plan for differentiation that transcend individual classrooms and grade levels. For example, if the gifted education specialist employs a problem-solving program or specialized mathematics program that can be implemented in grades K-5, then he or she spends less time planning different activities for individual classrooms. An added benefit to programs that span grade levels is that they allow for greater transfer of learning. Students progress through a comprehensive program over several years, completing every level of learning provided by the curriculum.

3. Programs are most effective when schools employ full-time gifted education specialists. Consultation and collaboration requires co-planning, co-teaching, and follow-up—a series of interactions occurring with every participating teacher and the gifted education specialist. Therefore, the overall number of teachers working with a given gifted education specialist is directly related to the amount and quality of these interactions. With too many teachers and too many different interactions, the gifted education specialist's efforts are spread too thin and allow little more than infrequent and superficial learning opportunities.

4. Clustering and ability grouping create an atmosphere that allows for the most effective use of resource consultation and collaboration processes. The frequency and quality of differentiated services depends upon the time the specialist has to engage designated teachers in collaboration and consultation. Therefore, when high-ability students are grouped together for instruction, fewer collaboration partnerships are necessary, and teachers can more frequently engage with the specialist again and again (Landrum, 2001). Further, the intellectual stimulation of groups of high-ability learners supports the academic and socio-emotional development of these students.

5. Educators must develop nonconsumable instructional materials whenever possible. Co-planning with several classroom teachers affords opportunities to develop differentiated activities appropriate to several classrooms. When the resources for these activities are nonconsumable, teachers and the gifted education specialist do not spend time developing new materials for repeated lessons for different students. Transportable centers or laminated student materials are helpful. Alternatively, students could be pulled together from various classrooms to use

materials in the gifted education specialist's room. This practice prevents several different regular classrooms from requiring the same materials.

6. The gifted education specialist should collect resource materials for students and/ or teachers and bring them into the regular classroom. Over time, classroom teachers become more able and willing to deliver differentiated lessons alone if they have the necessary materials at hand.

7. Establish specific criteria for selecting students for instructional groups. Most classroom teachers and gifted education specialists don't want sole responsibility for placing students in various instructional groups without accountability and documentation for that decision. So that placement becomes a match between identified need and lesson purpose, educators should collaboratively set criteria for placement in grouping formats and assess students based on these criteria. Educators should monitor student progress during instruction and make appropriate grouping placement changes as warranted.

8. Use inter- or multidisciplinary curricula to promote collaboration. Multidisciplinary or interdisciplinary curricula involve multiple subject areas in the curriculum, affording teachers opportunities to provide differentiated learning across more than one subject. If teachers compact lessons in several subject areas, they can open up more time for differentiation across several subject areas, thus facilitating more in-depth learning for target students.

9. Develop joint culminating activities that bring together general education and gifted learners. When the curricula for advanced learners and other classmates are related, students can share outcomes with one another during culminating activities. Although the levels of learning outcomes may vary, advanced learners can share what they have learned and model more sophisticated and complicated understandings for their classmates. However, assessment for grade-level and advanced learners for the culminating activity must be differentiated by using graduated rubrics for student products and/or performances.

In addition, the following guidelines are critical to program success (Landrum, 2001):

- Employ flexible student grouping practices (e.g., inter- and intraclassroom grouping, self-contained high-ability classes, etc.).
- Allow for flexible pacing of instruction for diverse student learners.
- Elicit administrative support for the program.
- Schedule periodic shared planning sessions for general and gifted educators.
- Schedule occasional long-term planning sessions (e.g. partial or full days).
- Ask for volunteer participation for collaboration.
- Provide quality differentiated learning opportunities for gifted learners.
- Provide training and follow-up technical support to staff members.
- Cluster gifted learners in a minimum number of classrooms with designated teachers.

Potential Pitfalls

Like any other educational practice, Resource Consultation and Collaboration Programs have potential obstacles to implementation. Knowing what to look out for will create a stronger program at the outset. Following are specific areas that can cause a Resource Consultation and Collaboration Program to falter or lose effectiveness.

Planning Sessions

The lack of common planning time for educational staff members poses a large threat to the efficacy of the program. Scheduling common instructional planning time for both the classroom teachers and the gifted education specialist is often difficult and may conflict with other policies or practices regarding the daily schedule. However, when grade level teachers do not meet periodically as a group, the gifted education specialist is forced meet with each teacher separately, which diminishes the time he or she has for instruction.

At a minimum, educators should set aside 30-45 minutes each week for planning sessions. The gifted education specialists can join common grade-level planning that already exists, or teachers can reschedule planning to include the gifted education specialist. Additionally, educators should set aside partial or full days each quarter to map out long-term planning for cooperative teaching. This overall plan for the quarter establishes a continuity in differentiated education opportunities over a period of time and allows educators to focus on specific lessons in weekly planning sessions.

Scheduling and Levels of Service

When the gifted education specialist's schedule becomes fixed or regimented, students can receive only a limited number of services. Likewise, if classroom teachers rely on gifted education specialists to provide frequent direct instruction to gifted learners, the program becomes limited to what only one or two individuals can do with students. One of the strengths of a Resource Consultation and Collaboration Program is that it draws classroom teachers and other staff into the roles of providing services to gifted learners. The gifted education specialist collaborates with classroom teachers and support staff to create those services, but he or she may not be directly involved in instruction. Relying less on direct instruction from the gifted education specialist and more on classroom teachers and other support staff allows the specialist to provide a wider variety of activities and opportunities for students when needs arise.

Lesson Preparation

There are two problems related to preparation that can impact the efficiency and efficacy of a Resource Consultation and Collaboration Program. First, if teachers across a given grade level don't share and recycle ideas and materials, the gifted education specialist is forced to duplicate his or her efforts for lesson planning, implementation, and student evaluation to cover the different classrooms. This extra time spent on preparation limits the overall frequency and duration of lessons delivered. To ease the burden on the gifted specialist and free his or her time for more instruction, classroom teachers must readily share ideas and materials with their colleagues.

Likewise, each advanced grade level and discipline that the specialist serves increases the required depth and breadth of curriculum that the specialist must learn, thus affecting the amount of time he or she can spend delivering services. At the elementary level, the curriculum presents a minimal challenge. However, at the middle school level more complex and sophisticated content is more of a challenge and requires more time. Gifted education specialists can alleviate some of the burden. First they can limit the number of grade levels or disciplines they serve. For example, if the general education program has provided provisions for raising the bar for gifted learners in math, then the specialist can and should focus on other disciplines. Second, a school can employ a variety of service delivery options at different grade levels. For example, all primary-aged students might be served by partial and full acceleration options rather than making individual accommodations for every child. Third, limiting the amount of direct contact the gifted specialist has with students (by providing more indirect and fewer direct services) minimizes the level of mastery of all content required by any given gifted education specialist. Finally, employing more than one gifted education specialist for any given staff allows the specialists to divide the disciplines and content they must master.

Materials and Resources

A shortage of instructional materials and other resources is frustrating and limiting in any learning environment, and a Resource Consultation and Collaboration Program can dramatically increase demands for materials and resources. Unlike traditional service delivery models in which a resource teacher implements one set of instructional activities at any given time, a Resource Consultation and Collaboration Program allows educators to implement multiple sets of activities within any one classroom as well as across many classrooms. For example, co-teaching or flexible student grouping often brings a large number of students together at one time, necessitating a large number of materials (e.g., novels) at once. Similarly, when teachers across a discipline or grade level use the same lessons at the same time, they require an increased number of materials.

In addition tó requiring a large number of materials, schools implementing a Resource Consultation and Collaboration Program will need access to a wide variety of instructional materials and other resources. The greater variety of instructional materials available, the more diverse the educational opportunities supported by the program become. Using materials from local and regional resources, as well as those provided at a distance through modern technology increases the diversity of activities provided to students. In addition, because quantity, quality, and variety are important, nonconsumable materials and those provided across levels or degrees of ability are very beneficial. Schools should take advantage of any regular education materials that allow for flexible pacing can be used for differentiated learning opportunities where and when necessary.

Facilities

A variety of instructional settings affect the collaborative process in a unique manner. Because Resource Consultation and Collaboration Programs require grouping students based on current intellectual performance and need, the make-up and size of the group changes with each lesson, potentially from one student to an entire classroom or larger. As a result, the space requirements for delivery of instruction can vary widely. Equally problematic is the fact that no one setting is appropriate for all instructional activities. One group of students might need research materials to complete an assignment while other students require laboratory equipment. Also important is the fact that multiple instructional activities may occur simultaneously. For example, one group of students might be engaged in small-group work, another student working on an independent study, and yet others working with a teacher. Although many teachers have grown accustomed to having multiple activities on-going at any given time in one setting, some have not.

Creating facilities conducive to resource consultation enhances the outcomes of the program, and the most important approach to using the physical makeup of classrooms is flexibility and creativity. All educators need to feel comfortable moving between classrooms and resource rooms and finding or creating appropriate spaces for instruction. For example, the gifted education specialist could work with target students in the classroom while a small group of students moves to the media center with the classroom teacher. Another option might be an appropriately designed room that divides space into separate areas (see prototype classroom examples in Chapter 7). In this setting, a small group of children can work with the teacher while another small group works at a center, and individual students work at computer stations with headsets. School staff should also keep in mind such alternative instructional settings as off-campus sites, media and technology centers, and language labs.

While schools and educators need to remain as flexible as possible when it comes to sharing rooms and space, it is important that the gifted education specialist maintain some permanent space. An unfortunate misperception about resource consultation, an approach that works closely with regular education, is that all activities must take place in the regular classroom, thereby denying the gifted education specialist any separate facilities. If the gifted education specialist does not have appropriate space of his or her own, he or she is restricted in the type and frequency of service delivery he or she can manage, thus limiting the program as a whole.

Grouping

Permanent heterogeneous grouping thwarts the efforts of a resource consultation program that employs a single gifted education specialist. If target students are spread across many classrooms for all instruction, the gifted education specialist must work harder to pool kids of like ability and needs for instructional purposes. In addition, when heterogeneous grouping spreads students across a large number of settings, it forces the specialist to repeat lessons with each different group. Likewise, when heterogeneous grouping creates smaller numbers of gifted learners in each setting, it limits the variety of instructional activities the group can do.

Developing flexible grouping policies and practices for students enhances the outcomes of the resource consultation program, contributing to the quality and quantity of differentiated learning opportunities. By grouping students within a finite set of classrooms, the specialist spends less time co-planning with teachers and more time developing activities for and working with students.

General Education Staff

The success of a Resource Consultation and Collaboration Program depends on the support and participation of the general education staff. Resource consultation typically requires more effort and time from the classroom teacher than more traditional formats for service delivery in gifted education. Classroom teachers must commit to regular co-planning sessions with the gifted education specialist, but if schedules are not built to support this time, then teachers perceive collaboration as one more burden added to their already loaded schedule. Likewise, classroom teachers need to view resource consultation efforts as consistent with and supportive of other educational initiatives. They must be able to fit resource consultation into their current regimen and point of view, or they may perceive resource consultation efforts as in opposition to other programs and policies.

Parental Support

As with any school program, lack of parental understanding and support can impede the success of a Resource Consultation and Collaboration Program. Therefore, building parent understanding and support is a component of any service delivery option in gifted education. Although more traditional gifted education programs target the parents of identified students alone, a Resource Consultation and Collaboration Program targets all advanced students, including non-identified students, who demonstrate a need for services. As a result, the base of parents who can provide support to the program is larger. A parent introduction and orientation to the program as well as consistent updates as a part of program maintenance are vital parts of a resource consultation program. Informal or formal meetings, written communication such as newsletters, and documentation of student work products are avenues for keeping parents informed about program activities.

Conclusion

Students are the real focus of a Resource Consultation and Collaboration Program. This program takes into account the reality that every student is different and provides a practical method for meeting the needs of students who, at any time, need more than the regular education curriculum provides them. As regular classroom teachers, gifted education specialists, administrators, and support staff work together for the common goal of providing students with activities and educational experiences that measure up to student abilities, classrooms become more than desks all in a row: they offer opportunities for students to rise to the challenges they are capable of meeting and become the future they have the potential to be.

References

Adams, L. & Cessna, K. (1991). Designing systems to facilitate collaboration: Collective wisdom from Colorado. *Preventing School Failure, 35* (4), 37-42.

Bauwens, J., Hourcade, J. J., & Friend, M. (1989). Cooperative teaching: A model for general and special education integration. *Remedial and Special Education, 10* (2), 17-29.

Cooke, L., & Friend, M. (1991). Principles of practice of consultation in schools. *Preventing School Failure, 35* (4), 6-9.

Curtis, M. J., Curtis, V. A., & Graden, J. L. (1988). Prevention and early intervention through intervention assistance programs. *School Psychology International, 9,* 257-264.

Curtis M. J., & Meyers, J. (1985). Best practices in school-based consultation. In A. Thomas & J. Grimes (Eds.), *Best Practices in School Psychology.* Washington, DC: National Association for School Psychologists.

Dettmer, P., Thurston, L. P., & Dyck, N. (1993). *Consultation, collaboration, and teamwork for students with special needs.* Boston, MA: Allyn & Bacon.

Dettmer, P., Thurston, L. P., & Dyck, N. (1999). *Consultation, collaboration, and teamwork for students with special needs* (second edition). Needham Heights, MA: Allyn & Bacon.

Donovan , A. (December, 1990). Team consultation. A presentation to York County Public Schools.

Landrum, M. S. (2001). An evaluation of the Catalyst Program: Consultation and collaboration in gifted education. *Gifted Child Quarterly, 45* (2), 139-151.

Tomlinson, C. A. (1995). *How to differentiate instruction in mixed-ability classrooms.* Alexandria, VA: ASCD.

Ward, S. B., & Landrum, M. S. (1994). *Resource consultation: An alternative service delivery model for gifted education. Gifted Child Quarterly, 16* (4), 272-279.

Wooster, J. (1978). *A handbook of strategies for differentiating instruction for gifted/ talented students.* Buffalo, NY: D.O.K.

REPRODUCIBLE FORMS

Planning Session Form
Lesson Planner
Student Differentiation Plan
Curriculum Planner
Lesson Modification Sheet
Gifted Education Specialist Planning Log
Monthly Consultation and Collaboration Form

Planning Session Form

Gifted Education Specialist Contact

Teacher:_____   Date:_____

Content Area(s): _____

_____

_____

Requests/Questions/Concerns: _____

_____

_____

_____

_____

_____

_____

_____

_____

_____

_____

_____

_____

_____

_____

_____

_____

_____

Lesson Planner

Theme: _____

Generalization: _____

Literature: _____

_____

Writing: _____

_____

Vocabulary: _____

_____

Art: _____

_____

Math: _____

_____

Science: _____

_____

Social Studies: _____

_____

Culminating Activity: _____

_____

Field Trips/Resources/Etc.: _____

_____

Evaluation:_____

_____

Timeline: _____

_____

Student Differentiation Plan

Student Name:_____   Grade Level:_____

Classroom Teacher:_____

Gifted Education Specialist:_____

Program Status: Non-gifted_____   Gifted_____

Strengths	Documentation	Differentiation
Math	____Pre-assessment ____85%ile Achievement ____Creative Problem Solver ____Critical Thinker ____Grades of A or B ____Proficiency Scores	
Communication	____Pre-assessment ____85%ile Achievement ____Creative Problem Solver ____Critical Thinker ____Grades of A or B ____Proficiency Scores	
Social Studies		
Science		

Discipline	September	October	November	December
Science				
Math				
Literature				
Communications				
Social Studies				
Interdisciplinary Units				
Interest Centers				

Differentiated Curriuclum Planner

Grade Level:_____

Lesson Modification Sheet			
Content	Process	Product	Learning Environment

Gifted Education Specialist Planning Log

Theme: _____

Grade Level: _____ Date: _____

Teachers Involved: _____

_____

Agenda: _____

_____

_____

_____

_____

_____

Accomplishments: _____

_____

_____

_____

_____

_____

To Be Completed: _____

_____

_____

_____

_____

_____

_____

Attach completed lesson plan when applicable.

Consultation and Collaboration Monthly Calendar

Directions: Record frequency with hatch marks (each mark equals an incidence of 1).

Type of Activity	Target Participants	Resources Used	Time Involved	Other
Types of Lessons ___Collaborative lesson ___Implement lesson ___Demonstration lesson ___Observation lesson ___Pull-out lesson ___Team-taught lesson	Gifted Students Served ___1-5 ___6-10 ___11-15 ___16-20 ___21-24 ___25+	Types of Instructional Materials ___Gifted program materials ___Personal materials ___Library materials ___Classroom materials ___Other general education materials ___Supplementary materials for use in regular classroom ___Other materials	Time for Initial Contact ___1-15 min. ___16-30 min. ___31-60 min. ___1-2 hrs. ___1/2 day ___full day	Comments:
Instructional Materials Development ___Pull-out materials ___Develop new materials ___Collect and desseminate materials	Non-gifted Students Served ___1-5 ___6-10 ___11-15 ___16-20 ___21-24 ___25+		Planning Time ___1-15 min. ___16-30 min. ___31-60 min. ___1-2 hrs. ___1/2 day ___full day	
Student Identification ___Assist in student assessment ___Attend eligibility meeting ___Conduct assessment	No. of Teachers Involved in Collaboration ___1 ___2-3 ___4+		Time for Implementation ___1-15 min. ___16-30 min. ___31-60 min. ___1-2 hrs. ___1/2 day ___full day	
Conferences ___Parent conference ___Student conference ___Teacher conference	Types of Collaboration ___by grade level ___one-on-one ___small group ___large group		Time for Follow-up ___1-15 min. ___16-30 min. ___31-60 min. ___1-2 hrs. ___1/2 day ___full day	